D1038853

Is It Antique Yet?

Frank Farmer Loomis IV

ALEXANDER Books

Founded 332 B.C.

a division of Creativity, Inc.

65 Macedonia Road
Alexander, NC 28701 USA
(704) 255-8719

™

Publisher: Ralph Roberts
Vice-President/Operations: Pat Hutchison Roberts

Senior Editor: Vivian Terrell
Production Editor: Barbara Blood

Cover Design: Gayle Graham
Cover Photography: Glenn Hartong
Interior Design & Electronic Page Assembly: **WorldComm**®
Photographs as indicated

Copyright ©1998 Frank Farmer Loomis IV

Reproduction and translation of any part of this work beyond that permitted by
Sections 107 and 108 of the United States Copyright Act without the permission
of the copyright owners is unlawful. Printed in the United States of America.

10 9 8 7 6 5 4 3 2

Library of Congress Cataloging-in-Publication

Loomis, Frank Farmer, 1949-
      Is it antique yet? / Frank Farmer Loomis IV.
            p. cm.
      ISBN 1-57090-034-5
      1. Antiques.   I. Title.
      NK1125.L66   1997
      745. 1--dc21   97-33985
                                                                                  CIP

The author and publisher have made every effort in the preparation of this book to ensure the
accuracy of the information. However, the information in this book is sold without warranty,
either express or implied. Neither the author nor Alexander Books will be liable for any damages
caused or alleged to be caused directly, indirectly, incidentally, or consequentially by the
information in this book.

The opinions expressed in this book are solely those of the author and are not necessarily
those of Alexander Books.

Trademarks: Names of products mentioned in this book known to be or suspected of
being trademarks or service marks are capitalized. The usage of a trademark or service
mark in this book should not be regarded as affecting the validity of any trademark or
service mark.

Alexander Books™—a division of Creativity, Inc.—is a full–service publisher located at
65 Macedonia Road, Alexander NC 28701. Phone (704) 252–9515, Fax (704) 255–8719.
For orders only: 1-800-472-0438. Visa and MasterCard accepted.

Alexander Books™ is distributed to the trade by Midpoint Trade Books, Inc., 27 West
20th Street, New York NY 10011, (212) 727-0190, (212) 727-0195 fax.

This book is also available on the internet in the **Publishers CyberMall.** Set your browser to
http://www.abooks.com and enjoy the many fine values available there.

CONTENTS

DEDICATION:

To my publisher:
  Mr. Ralph Roberts and
    his wonderful staff
My supportive friends and particularly:
  Andrew Balterman
  Donna Burns
  Anita J. Ellis
  Stephen L. Fletcher
  Grace K. Hill
  Rose Huber
  Clare Walsh and Roland E. Johnson
  Karen M. Keane
  Dianne and Peter Marcus
  Debbie and Cliff Radel
  William Santen, Sr.
  Vivian Terrell
  Douglas Tillson
  James H. Whitaker
My sister:
  Deborah Loomis Bigelow
Our antiquer aunt:
  Frances Loomis Wilson
And her mother and our gram:
  Frances LaRocque Lennon who gave me
    my first antique, taught me to be a
    gentleman, and whose whole life gave
    me love.

FOREWORD
Clement E. Conger

Frank Farmer Loomis in **Is It Antique Yet?** writes about antiques with freshness and enthusiasm. He tackles a subject that has often been treated in staid and sometimes humorless volumes destined to remain on coffee tables. This is a book to keep handy, to read again and again.

The information presented is very interesting. The writing is energetic, no flowery sentences but is useful and explained with straightforward facts. All this makes learning about antiques entertaining and effortless. His down-to-earth teaching gives the beginners and advanced collectors a fine foundation for antiques.

Mr. Loomis brings to life the heroes and heroines of the antiques world. How fascinating to learn that Josiah Wedgwood occasionally decorated his ceramics with political messages. Mrs. Abraham Lincoln during the Civil War, through her decorating, tried to make the White House as elegant as Buckingham Palace.

Thomas Chippendale is rightfully given his proper due as a superb cabinet maker. No true lover of antiques could argue against the author calling the Queen Anne style "the eternal star of antiques."

As antiques soar in value, Mr. Loomis has some welcome suggestions for getting more antiques for your money. Best of all, he emphasizes a point that is too often overlooked, the excitement and exhilaration antiques bring. I remember happily seeing the smiling visitors touring the White House and State Department Rooms awed by being reminded of our American Heritage of the fine and decorative arts. Mr. Loomis constantly shows us how collecting antiques can better our lives.

Clement E. Conger,
Retired Curator of:
the White House, 1970-1986
the Diplomatic Rooms at the
    State Department, 1961-1992
the Blair House, 1976-1992

1

Is It Antique Yet?

Welcome to the world of antiques. *Is It Antique Yet?* and yours truly are your coaches into an antiques lifestyle that adds much positivism to our lives. The best and easiest way to learn is to start right at the beginning. In our case we need to know exactly the meaning of the term "antique." It is often confusing, over-used, and rarely defined. Rest assured this book is nothing like a computer manual. Everything will be explained in an easy nonintimidating manner that will build your self-confidence, get you totally hooked, and enhearten your hankering for more understanding.

Before we get into all that historic jargon, let me tell you how I learned to find out if it is antique yet.

After a speech about antiques to a service club, I was questioned by a nonantiquer gentlemen who asked me, quite seriously, "Do they still make antiques?" Not only did his query bring the house down, but it also made me realize how misunderstood the word antique really is.

Even though the exact definition of antique is often confusing, the mere mention of the word can really stir our emotions. How many of us, for example, can visualize Grandma in her ancient rocking chair or peeling apples at her old-fashioned kitchen cabinet? How many of the dishes, utensils, and other pieces Grandma used then are today considered antiques?

How many of us are crushed to think we gave away antique items at our last garage sale or how proud we are to have bought

Photograph courtesy of Skinner, Inc.

These items dating from Egyptian and Roman times go back to 600 years before Christ, and are called "Antiquities." This word is the basis of the expression "antiques."

an antique for a song from an unknowing seller?

We need some approachable definitions. Doesn't that sound more user-friendly and totally uncomputer-manualish than saying less constraining ones?

So here they are:

Definition 1: The Purist Definition of Antique

This one is called the traditional approach. Let's discuss the once universally accepted definition of antique.

Before the 1880s, antique referred to items made during the glory days of the ancient world, which included Egypt, Rome, and Greece. That term is still in use today. When an auction sells items such as statuary from the ancient world they usually choose the word antiquities to describe the sale.

Around 1880, the purist definition evolved, meaning "an antique was any item made before 1820." Why 1820? That year marks the general beginning of the Industrial Revolution in both Western Europe and the United States. After 1820, most furniture, silver, and china, which had previously been hand-made, was produced by machinery. This 1820s rule is the elite definition for antiques because most items in this group today are too expensive for many of us.

These European ceramics from the 1600s and 1700s date long before 1820.

This date also incorrectly assumes that because an item is handmade, it is of better quality than a comparable machine-manufactured one. Remember, age and being handmade are not synonymous with quality. Junk is junk whether handmade in 1820 or 1907. Just spell it "junque" to make it seem ritzier if it is made before 1820 in order to satisfy the purists.

Finding affordable pre-1820 antiques is truly demanding and needs much luck and time for looking, as well as a fat checkbook. There is little doubt that buying such pricey items can create much tension such as worrying about having paid too much? This exclusive group has record-breaking price tags. A top-of-the-line chest of drawers from 1780, for instance, could cost more than the average house! So that is definition one.

Another example of a pre-1820 antique is this oak English chest of drawers from the 1600s.

Photograph courtesy of Skinner, Inc.

Photograph courtesy of Skinner, Inc.

When this animated bull dog from 1900 turns 100, Uncle Sam will consider it a genuine antique.

Definition 2: Uncle Sam's Definition of Antique

In contrast to the purist notion, Uncle Sam offers us a downright friendlier and less restrictive definition for antiques. The United States Customs Office says items must be 100 years old or older to enter the United States duty free as a genuine antique. Unlike the 1820s definition, this one obviously changes yearly, allowing more items to qualify, and it is generally a good one for us to follow.

Thus a 100-year-old silver tea service is now considered antique, but ten years ago Uncle Sam would not have labeled it as a genuine antique. Even though the government has a rather liberal definition for antique, it is still too restrictive. We need a more open ruling.

Antiques collecting has become quite chic. Just check out all the antiques malls popping up in the downtown areas of smaller towns across the United States. Antique items, in fact, are as in as low-fat foods and bottled water. But unlike bottled water, which is likely to be replaced by another voguish beverage at some future point, it appears that antiques collecting is a national addiction. Thankfully, antiquing is here to stay.

Because of the immense popularity of antiquing, the scope of the definition needs to be broadened a little more than either Uncle Sam's or the traditionalists' rules dictate.

Definition 3: The Loomis Definition of Antique

Here is what I humbly call a "*Loomism*." An antique is any item made before 1915. Why that year? Because World War I marked the end of an era. After the death of Queen Victoria in 1901, the world languished during the first decade of the twentieth century. By the finish of World War I the old ways were ending which included everything from lifestyles to clothing.

By the 1920s, the modern, high-tech world we know today was developing at full speed. Just look at photos of vintage 1910ish ladies. Their frocks, loaded with lace, had long billowy skirts. Within a few years, this Victorian look would give way to the streamlined and sleek flapper outfits associated with the roaring twenties. Those fashions illustrated how the world had radically changed after the first fifteen years of the twentieth century. Thus, items dating from around or before 1915 can truly be considered antiques. That opens up many goodies for us to call antiques.

Besides referring to an old-fashioned era, my 1915 definition presents another argument–the delicate age question. What one person considers old, another finds relatively new.

Photographs courtesy of Skinner, Inc.

Golden Oak pieces such as this pre-1915 oak dining table and sideboard are popular antiques.

Photograph courtesy of Skinner, Inc.

Beatles memorabilia will become genuine antiques and so will this dime bank from the 1964-1965 New York World's Fair.

Generally speaking, a person's prejudiced interpretation of old in antiques depends upon his or her age and geographical location within the United States.

Think of it this way: when someone is eighteen, someone thirty is (in kind terms) middle aged. But by the time that eighteen-year-old is eyeballing twenty-eight, then thirty seems quite youthful. Translated into antiquese, for today's very young collector, 1960s Beatles memorabilia may seem ancient. Yet, to the more mature, these items reminiscent of the "Fab Four" are viewed as rather modern.

Geography has a similar effect upon a person's view of what is antique and what is not. On the East Coast for instance, the earliest, non-native American antiques of European styling usually date from the 1600s when settlement by the white man began. There is a constant awareness that old can be 300 years or more. Thus exhibits and shows in New York, Boston, or Charleston are more likely to exhibit pre-1820 antiques than the rest of the country.

According to the rest of the USA, however, our 1915 Loomism really makes sense. Midwestern cities such as Chicago, founded in 1803, Louisville in 1779, and Cincinnati

in 1788, are really babies when compared to their East Coast
urban cousins.

Collectors in the Midwest are like a thirty-year-old regarding forty as old. Antiques seem to become younger the farther
west we go. Collectors in relatively newer cities such as Denver,
settled in 1857, Dallas in 1841, and Seattle in 1852, are like the
twenty-year-old viewing thirty as ancient.

A 1780 chair, an 1810 pewter teapot, or even an 1680
blanket chest (all examples of the traditional definitions of
antiques) are more likely to turn up in an east coast shop than
a west coast one. Shopping in younger California offers more
twentieth-century delicacies such as 1910 glassware or Nippon
china vases from Japan.

Photograph courtesy of Skinner, Inc.

Furniture replicating earlier styles such as 1920s pieces are now semi-
antiques and will mature as genuine antiques.

Photograph courtesy of Skinner, Inc.

This Wedgwood plaque from 1977 answers that perplexing question: do they still make antiques? Indeed, this will someday be an antique.

Our 1915 *Loomism* opens many affordable purchases for us without stretching the antique question too much. Besides, if you really love the piece, who cares how old it is? Remember quality is far more important than age.

When visiting shops or malls, we often find 1925 merchandise such as oak kitchen cupboards or 1950s movie magazines with Marilyn on the cover. So, what do we label those goodies and the myriad others from the 1930s and 1940s such as pink or green Depression Glass, Grandma's good set of French china, and our Fiestaware? After all, these items may hold precious memories of departed loved ones and happy times. Call these types semi-antiques. Shops and malls are full of wonderful semi-antiques that offer great value and quality. They are usually just as well-made as their ancestors and their youth makes them less costly. Check out 1930s china, 1920s tea carts, and 1940s radio cabinets. In time, these semi-antiques will graduate into being full-time antiques, and the *Loomism* will need updating.

Here is a real example of how affordable and terrific semi-antiques are. Would you believe $54 for a mahogany hand needlepoint footstool from the 1940s? Do you think I paid too much?

Whether 1700s cherry is your cup of tea or 1930s chrome is your bag, use our definitions of antique and semi-antique to define your collecting. And thank goodness we don't all want to collect the same stuff! Think of how expensive and boring everything would become. The choice is yours–to each their own.

Be sure to remember one more thing. The gentleman who asked if they still make antiques is right. Difficult as it may be to comprehend, many of the quality items being turned out today such as handmade quilts and hooked rugs will indeed, someday, be considered antiques.

For the time being, however, let's get started on our self-study antiques course and learn some of the advantages antiques offer. The next chapter will show you how antiques can brighten drab surroundings and enliven spirits.

2

The Advantages of Antiques

N ow that the definitions of antiques have been demystified, a look into why we get addicted to them is our next step. Why do we collect antiques? What advantages do they offer? Here are the main motives.

Reason 1: More for Your Money

Antiques offer a lot more for our bucks. Recently this antiquer paid $165 for semi-antique patio furniture complete with a glass-topped table and four chairs. All it needed was a sanding to remove the rust and then a couple of coats of spray paint. Not bad when a new set similar to mine may cost upwards of $500. Antiques give us more for our money which is more important now than ever.

Reason 2: Quality

Here's another advantage antiques have over comparable new items: old is usually better made. Check the carving on an antique chair. Now compare it to similar decoration on a brand-new chair. Notice how crisp, almost three dimensional the old is while the new is flatter, almost one dimensional. Rub your hands over both of them to feel the difference between new and old. Old is usually better and more affordable. That brand-new chair probably sells in a store for more than the antique one. Not all new items lack quality, but the best is usually astronomically high.

Photograph courtesy of Skinner, Inc..

Wind up this metal European music box from the late 1800s, and a little singing bird pops out.

Reason 3: Holds Up in Value

Another advantage is that antiques retain their value and perhaps in time will even increase in worth. Remember that is true only if we bought them at a good price and kept them for awhile. If we could go back in time and compare 1970s prices versus today's, it would be easy to understand. For instance, I bought a French clock in Paris in the early 1970s for the then-to-me astronomical cost of $25. Today it would probably bring $300 at auction. I don't care if it is worth fifty cents because I love it for its curlicue charm and as a remembrance of a wonderful day in Paris. It is nice to know you may someday monetarily profit from your antiques, but still collect them because you love them.

Here is more proof that it is prudent to purchase antiques whenever possible rather than contemporary items. New belongings don't hold onto their value as oldies. The second you take your purchase out of a store, it is suddenly used merchandise. Have you ever had a garage sale and tried to sell a sofa or dinette set that is just six months young? You are lucky if you get twenty-five percent of what you paid for it.

Reason 4: Sentimentality

Toss aside the monetary advantages and grab the best reason of all to collect antiques: their sentimental value. If you

Photograph courtesy of Skinner, Inc.

Pets and antiques go hand in hand. This charming scene attributed to
Alfred Arthur Brunel de Neuville (French 1852-1941) entitled "The Bowl
of Milk," brings out the cat lover in us.

are lucky enough to have family pieces, take a look at one.
Perhaps it was your great-grandmother's rocking chair. Caress
the arm rests. Just think of the times this chair has seen. Perhaps
an ancestor was nursed in it or sat there nervously knitting while
waiting for news about her son fighting at Gettysburg.

The sentimental value of antiques is perhaps the most
magnetic reason for their adoration. If you are about to acquire
your very first, it will be a thrill. Let your imagination create an
emotional story for your new-to-you antique. Or perhaps you
may be fortunate enough to find one with a documented history.

All this talk about the psychological aspect of antiques
brings up an important term that has to do with sentimentality:
provenance. This comes from the French meaning, "from the
source." Think of provenance as the antique's ancestry.

It is the history of the rocking chair passing from one
generation to the next, who sat there, and who courted whom
from that chair. When the provenance includes a famous
person or an event, the value of the item can go through the

A carousel horse, attributed to Allan Herschell, of New York, recalls that old fashioned amusement ride.

Photograph courtesy of Skinner, Inc..

roof. How do you think that expression "George Washington slept here" got started? Probably by some inventive real estate agent trying to sell a "fixer-upper" by giving it some sales appeal. In a later chapter we shall further discuss provenance. So treasure your antiques for all the good vibrations from the past they bring to you.

Reason 5: Fun to Acquire

If sentimentality does not get you on the antiques band-wagon, here is another sure-fire reason. Antiques can be a bonding experience among people. We can become even better friends by antiquing with our favorite people. Mark, a

Photograph courtesy of Skinner, Inc..

Glass decorations from the early 1900s add an old-time sparkle to the holidays.

Photograph courtesy of Skinner, Inc.

This tin wind-up biplane from the 1900s keeps alive a happy childhood.

single father, uses antiques outings as a way to have quality time with his son Bryson. That young man some day is going to be a serious antiquer and will fondly remember times spent antiquing with his dad. And quite possibly not too far off he will lament "those cheap prices when I was a kid." Of course that is if prices keep going up on antiques as they have been doing for a long time.

Reason 6: Antiquing is Just Plain Fun

There is some corny old song that Judy Garland sings that goes something like: "So forget your troubles, come on get happy," and I always add, "and let's go antiquing." Rummaging aisle after aisle at a mall or show is just plain "forgetting everything." Try it. All your troubles and stresses will disappear while you are shopping. You're on a minivacation. Just looking at your favorites such as cranberry glass from the 1890s or colorful 1915 quilts can boost your morale.

One word of caution: If you have written too many checks because you have purchased too much, that can create much tension. Take it from the voice of experience from this antiquer and be careful.

Although this doll from the late 1800s sheds tears when she is "wound up," she is still a hoot.

Photograph courtesy of Skinner, Inc..

Reason 7: History Lesson

There is no better teacher for understanding the past than antiques. They are more enlightening than any history book. Have you ever wondered why most mid-1800s chairs have castors only on the front legs? Those small wheels made it easier to move furniture in order to take carpets outside for cleaning. Today's vacuums make housekeeping easier, and furnishings tend to stay in one place. Hence most modern chairs lack castors.

Why were the castors only on the two front legs and none on the back? They made it easier for the sitter to scoot the chair closer to a warming fire or perhaps to be nearer to someone for an intimate conversation. Four castors would make the chair slide like roller skates. Antiques give us an idea of how our ancestors courted using those little wheels for more intimate experiences.

Reason 8: Positivism

Talking about antiques shows, especially outdoor ones, brings up the subject of our canine associates. Ever notice how many antiquers take their dogs along to outdoor shows or how dealers have their best friend with them in their booths? Sometimes it's hard to tell who is enjoying the event more, the humans or the pooches.

The artist Alexander Pope, (American 1849-1924) known for pictures of dogs, in "Portrait of a Setter," captures a beloved canine.

Photograph courtesy of Skinner, Inc..

Antiques have another wonderful trait, and it has the same soothing effect as our pets. Medical experts tell us the healthy facts about pets. Just having a dog or cat we love can lower our blood pressure or reduce stress in our lives. There is no argument about that. Add one more ingredient to this stress reduction recipe that medical experts may just be beginning to acknowledge: antiques.

Imagine this: After a miserable day, all seems far worse than really is. In this highly strung antiquer's case I jog a couple very slow miles. Afterwards, life looks less serious but glumness is still present. When everything else fails to put a smile on your face, try this. Put your favorite antique, such as a picture or a vase, in a spot in your home where it will greet you as you open the door. I can't tell you how often (more times than I care to admit) I've been mad at the world and even angrier at myself. Then I walked into the kitchen after a day of misery, and there were my 1860s Blue Willow platters. Wow! How those platters with their white background and blue pagodas and lovebirds always cheer me. The next time you have had a less-than-perfect day, see how antiques lovingly bolster you.

So here we have the eight main reasons for collecting antiques. You are probably saying to yourself this Loomis guy is an antiques fanatic. I gladly and with gratitude admit that. To prove my objectivity about antiques, we shall go over their disadvantages.

Photograph courtesy of Skinner, Inc..

Imagine the rush looking at this oil depicting flowers by Gamaliel Waldo Beaman (American 1852-1937) could bring to us on a nonstop rainy day or night.

After great efforts, this antiquer tried to come up with one disadvantage about antiques. Most antique furniture, silver, and china are more ornate than new. This means they require more dusting than modern furnishings. It really does take more effort to dust all those curlicues. While doing it, you are getting to know your antiques even better because you can't help but notice how the pieces of a table were put together. So that positive effect renders what I thought might be a disadvantage into an advantage.

Antiques have no disadvantages and are not even fattening. In the next chapter learn how to get the most antique dash without much cash.

3

More Antiques Dash for Our Cash

Are you beginning to feel like a real antique pro, oops, or rather should we say a real antiques professional? Here is a funny point about antiques. You are reading an antiques book not an antique book. Yours truly is an antiques appraiser who is rapidly becoming an antique appraiser. The next time you go antiquing look around and see how many "antique" shops and malls there are when they really should be called "antiques" malls or shops. Antique is the adjective meaning old and the word antiques is a noun meaning all those pre-1915 items waiting to be collected. So this chapter is appropriately called "getting more antiques dash for our cash" or "the most antique dash for our cash." It is up to you on this one.

Photograph courtesy of Skinner, Inc.

The provenance of these Chippendale style ladder-back mahogany and walnut armchairs states, "Deaccessioned from a Connecticut museum." That means a museum is selling antiques from its collection which makes the item "museum quality," and more expensive.

Photograph courtesy of Skinner, Inc.

Buying matched sets of anything is more expensive. This suite of English Queen Anne chairs will cost more per chair than four unmatched chairs.

Shopping is the most enjoyable part of antiques. Perhaps you will be getting your first antique or you will be adding to family pieces. It does not make any difference. Together we are about to experience "the sport of successful antiques shopping" as we toss aside daily tensions and cares.

Forget any mistaken idea that you cannot afford antiques.

This chapter is full of recommendations that are as easy as buttering toast.

You are more primed for this adventure than you realize. We now know what an antique is, a fine foundation for becoming successful antiquers. It is something like being a first-time jogger. You have just jogged that long first mile, which in our case was learning how to define antiques. Perhaps you have heard or experienced the "runner's high." We are about to have an "antiquer's high," the result of getting beautiful objects for much less dough than we ever thought possible.

Two Types of Antiquers

Now we have to be a little intense. It is necessary to divide us antiquers into two different groups. Remember whichever you choose the other ones are still in our antiques community. The first type of collector wants antiques in pristine condition, and fortunately for them, cost is not a major concern. They are blessed because they can match their champagne tastes with their Moet and Chandon budgets. They can afford the best pieces such as 1740s Queen Anne highboys. And when they collect newer antiques dating from the late 1800s or early 1900s, they are usually very upscale, such as 1910 Tiffany stained-glass lamps or 1880s ornate furniture by the Herter Brothers of New York City. They can also buy what is currently considered fashionable (usually at high prices because chicness brings more zeros to the price) such as 1910 angular Craftsman furniture by Gustav Stickley.

The second troupe, however, has slimmer wallets and possess much self-confidence, resulting in highly individualistic antiquers. They buy what they like and do not give a hoot about what is "hot." Neither condition, age, nor trendiness is as crucial as it is for the first group. This attitude gets more antiques for the buck. So read on to get the know-how.

If you are not part of the first group, do not despair. Who really has extra money these days for high-end antiques? My affectionate nickname for the second brood is the "free-spirited fun set." Yours truly considers himself a charter member because my pals always remind me that an upscale antique for me is anything over $35. Be a member of this society, too. It promises many affordable antiques. You will be amazed who were early role models for this clever set, but that information will come later.

Buy Semi-antiques

You already know the first trick. Remember that 1915 antiques and those semi-antiques made from the 1920s and onwards were mass-produced and are still plentiful. Therefore, they are less costly than antiques that are 100 years or older. Earlier pieces are not available because they were either individually crafted or produced in smaller quantities by early machines. So there you have it: purchase antiques or semi-antiques which date after 1915. You will save a bundle on those younger items, and the quality is still there. Always remember, age is no guarantee for excellence, which is the most important trait for any antique.

Canvass those semi-antiques. Go to local antiques malls to find early twentieth-century versions of older styles. A 1935 replica of a Sheraton-style 1810 dining chair is a good example. The younger one truly resembles its ancestor. Both pieces have reddish mahogany wood, rounded legs, and square-shaped backs, all trademarks of this 1790s furniture designer. Would you believe $150 versus $1,500 or more for the real McCoy? Do not neglect those semi-antiques. They give us a lot more value and offer practically line for line the same good looks and craftmanship as their antique counterparts.

Let's avoid calling semi-antiques "collectibles" because it sets up an image of tube socks at flea markets.

Buy Unfashionable

Here is another point about the power that arrives from being an independent collector. You usually get more value when you buy what is not fashionable. Blue and white china is a good example. It seems there are a lot of us who are crazy about the Willow pattern on china. Decorating magazines are full of articles glorifying this English ceramic dating from the mid to late 1800s. Did you know Willoware was made in other combinations? It is the blue and white that is the most fashionable. Of course, along with stylishness comes priciness. So be a rugged individualist and avoid the trendies and collect what you like but perhaps with a twist.

In this case it means buying Willow in a nonblue combination. Why not try green, brown, yellow, or pink? The savings can be as much as sixty percent for the same quality, but no blue. Do not worry; those pagodas and lovebirds look just as endearing in other hues. Everyone can have blue and white Willow, but how many homes display pink and white renditions? Your home will be truly unique with some nice pieces, and you will have some funds left for other goodies.

A little bit of "Frankness" is due here. In all honesty, the other combinations do not cut it for this antiquer. As an appraiser I suggest the other colors, but as a collector only blue and white will do for me. Do you recall when we discussed how antiques de-stress our lives? As I said earlier, that divine blue

Photograph courtesy of Skinner, Inc.

Buy a style that is less popular and you will get a better value. This William and Mary style highboy from the early 1700s is usually less costly than a comparable Queen Anne one.

and white Willow is the first thing this highly strung gentleman sees upon entering his home. Especially after a trying day, to me it portrays beautiful tranquility. That blue and white artistic union is my addiction. If you are hooked, too, keep reading. In a little while there will be some suggestions on how to find that magic duo at friendlier prices.

This strategy about buying only what you like is also wise with furniture. Buy styles that are not in vogue. This is especially true about pre-1820 pieces that are naturally costlier in the first place.

Try to avoid antiques that never seem to get unpopular, and you may end up with some bargains. The superb Queen Anne style from the early to mid-1700s with its curved cabriole leg is sumptuous but incredibly expensive for most of us. Why? Unlike other antique styles, it has practically enjoyed nonstop adoration. Even people who think they don't like antiques probably sit upon a rendition of a Queen Anne style wing chair. So how do you get something reasonable from that era? Buy the earlier generation of English furniture. It was named after King William and Queen Mary who ruled in the late 1600s. The

William and Mary style is in less demand than Queen Anne; therefore, it costs less. Antiques snobs may say the older style is somewhat chunkier with its ice-cream-cone-shaped legs, but nonetheless it is still lovely and well made.

Thumbing through the pages of an auction catalogue is a practical lesson in how to get more antiques for our bucks. Skinner's of Boston often auctions late 1600s and early 1700s furniture. A comparison between prices fetched for English lowboys (pieces about the size of small serving tables with three or four drawers) is a good lesson about value. A William and Mary lowboy most times will fetch fifty percent less than a comparable Queen Anne. This also shows that old does not necessarily mean more expensive. So when looking for a certain antique piece of furniture, choose something in another style because it may offer you more value.

Buy "Problems"

Besides being very individualistic, the free-spirited antiquers fret less about condition than the first group. Buying less-than-perfect antiques allows us to get pre-1820 goodies without emptying our pocketbooks.

English tea caddies from the 1700s were used as small wooden safes (complete with a lock) to guard precious tea leaves. These antiques in pristine condition can be pretty costly.

When this tea caddy from the 1790s is displayed with the lid open, no one can see its missing veneer. (inset below)

Photographs courtesy of Glenn Hartong.

Photograph courtesy of Garth's Auction.

Take a look at these two lowboys. The one on the left is cherry, refinished, original handles, with only minor repairs. The right lowboy is mahogany, replaced handles and top, with a reworked front. It is hard to tell the difference between the two, both date from the mid 1700s. The left lowboy sold at Garth's Auction in 1990 for $5,000, the right one sold in 1996 for $935. Only an expert can spot the "problems" in the right one. Buying less than "mint condition" oldies gives us more antiques dash for our cash.

Glance at the photo of one. It does look in pretty good condition, doesn't it? Let's turn it around, and ahah! There is some veneer missing. That is bad for the tea caddy and the first set of antiquers, but wonderful news for us. Why? A similar caddy, if in first-class condition, would probably run about $750. This one could be picked up for a song, about half the amount of the good one, just because some veneer is missing. Other than the first group of collectors, who really cares about that so called defect? Just place it where no one can see its "problem." How could something that has been around since 1790 (even with the best of care) be without a few imperfections?

By now maybe you are part of the second group of antiquers. We are not excessively picky about condition. The more scratches, dents, and chips the better. After all, part of the charm of antiques is that they have been kissed by time.

Here are some tips on how to get the most china for your antiques dollar. Plate hangers and tall bookcases are a china collector's best friend. If you collect 1820s blue and white

This Wedgwood vase from the 1950s has two small chip in its base. Oh well, no one can really see them.

Photograph courtesy of Glenn Hartong.

English pieces depicting American historical scenes, be prepared to spend upwards of $400. That's per plate and in excellent condition, meaning nothing wrong. How about spending seventy-five percent less for one?

Here is the secret. Buy plates with "problems." Just hang those early American scenes made by famous English potteries such as Spode or Wedgwood high on a wall. Use a plate hanger or place them on the top shelf of a bookcase for everyone to admire. The secret is to admire them at a d-i-s-t-a-n-c-e. Soon even you will not see the chips or cracks. Only the seductive combination of blue and white will be noticed.

After suggesting Willoware in color combinations other than blue and white, you were told about my addiction to this historical combination. My collection has small imperfections but it is in that charming color team. Whether made by top-of-the-line English Royal Doulton or in Japan in the 1930s, flawed Willow is usually sold for about fifty percent or less than those in good condition. So this antiquer's Willow is all diplomatically displayed on top shelves of bookcases or on walls close to the ceilings. Their less-than-perfect condition barely shows. Finding defective Willow offers the best of both worlds: the blue and white pattern but thankfully at a more affordable price.

That same "less than perfect" rule also works well with paintings if you are longer on empty wall space than cash. When purchasing an oil by a well-known artist, expect to pay a hefty price for one in good condition.

Just as real estate agents label houses for sale needing repairs as "fixer-uppers," it is the same with old paintings. The next time you go antiquing look in the corners or back rooms of shops, galleries, or malls for your artwork. Retailers don't prominently display "as is" pictures.

When you find one you like but it has a small tear or needs cleaning, follow the "hang them high rule" used with chipped china. Place them in spots that do not allow a viewer a too-close inspection. Paintings are meant to be seen and admired from afar. It is probably true that those three French monarchs, Louises XIV, XV, and XVI had some tattered canvases at their palace, Versailles. The "Sun King," Louis XIV, knew the esthetic advantages of high ceilings when he constructed his chateau outside Paris back in the late 1600s.

In time it is smart to have the pictures professionally restored. In the meantime, touch up the bruises on the frames with similar gold paint. After you have finally had the paintings restored, you probably still saved about fifty percent of the price of first-class condition.

Photograph courtesy of Skinner, Inc.

Monogrammed anything, especially silver flatware or a tea service, offers us more antiques for our buck.

Buy Anonymity

Scanning through catalogues of paintings to be auctioned can really teach us much about getting more oomph for our money. Your eyes spot two pictures by two different artists beckoning you. Either one would look gorgeous in your living room, and both are in good condition. Even the frames are similar. Yet one sold for five times the amount of the other. What is the difference between them? Why is one so much more expensive? The explanation is basically hype. The difference between the two is similar to the gaps in costs between Toyota's models of Camry and Lexus automobiles. The costlier Lexus has leather seats and instant recognition as a status vehicle. The other similar looking and usually with less costly upholstery Camry is no less dependable but is considered more "middle of the road."

The paintings' values at auction are similar to the hoopla of automobiles. The artist of the first is a "Lexus" among painters. They are listed in art reference books such as *Leonard's* and have a history of selling at auctions and galleries for thousands. The signature is instantly recognizable by those who think they are in the know about art. On the other hand, the "Camry" artist has sold very little at auction and is rather unknown. Who cares? This gem sold for much less, which makes it more reachable to us collectors. Perhaps in time this artist's efforts will become well-known. Does status make a painting any more beautiful? Only to the insecure!

The only thing less valuable than a painting by a second-tier artist (a genteel way of saying it is in the Camry price range) is an unsigned one. An anonymous canvas is like a field of wild flowers. Few seem to appreciate their "ungreenhouse" aura but those who do are truly fortunate. It is the same with a canvas that is considered second rate because it lacks an autograph. Its unauthenticated charm is there for discovery by the second group of collectors who have faith in their own judgment.

Here is this penny-pinching antiquer's story about a recently purchased anonymous painting. When I visit my sister in

Michigan, we always go to one of our favorite antiques shops, William Lesterhouse, in Mattawan. The proprietor is totally honest. When Bill says something is "Wedgwood, circa 1880" it is. He has downright terrific prices. On a snowy February outing with Debbie, we visited Bill's shop. She bought some blue and white Wedgwood plates, and I "stole" an enticing landscape.

As we walked into his store, there it was on a side wall— a stunning summer landscape of trees, sun, mountains, and a river. It was done in a very realistic manner and encased in an ornate (not too bordelloish) gold frame. It was fine quality and had that mid-1800s almost photographic realistic look. Bill said it was a "Hudson River Valley scene from about 1850 to 1875." Those 1800s scenes highlighting the Hudson River as it flowed in upstate New York are extremely pricey these days. Collectors love them because they are a slice of Americana. Bill offered it for $325. How come so little you ask? The reason: few collectors wanted it because it lacked its "John Hancock."

This antiquer was thrilled. If it had been signed by Thomas Cole (1801-1848), it could have fetched more than $950,000 at auction. If labeled by a second tier painter it might have been in the "Camry" class selling for several thousand. Also it probably would have sold before we ever met because signed art, although more expensive, sells quicker. The really chuckling part of this story is that sometimes I follow my advice too closely. It automatically got hung in a very high spot over the mantel in the den so that after a long winter day it can be ogled from the sofa. You are probably saying I am really not used to having canvases in good condition. How true! It really could have been placed anywhere. You are now thinking like fun antiquers. So try to buy unsigned artwork.

Someday it would be nice to figure out why some artists did not sign their works. Was it humility or perhaps their names were accidentally removed when a picture was cleaned? Oh well, we should be grateful because anonymous works give us so much wildflower beauty that we might not be able to afford if they were signed. That should please those humble masters.

A few years ago this print from the 1880s was purchased in Paris for less than two dollars!

Photograph courtesy of Glenn Hartong.

Buy New Frames

Here is an easy tip about paintings. Just as a lousy tie can ruin a suit, so can a frame. A more flattering frame is a reasonable way to put the finishing touches on a painting. So if you are not crazy about the frame, try a different one. An antique frame or one from your favorite framer can make your painting look like it came from the Louvre.

Buy Prints

While we are mentioning that glorious gallery, pretend you are in Paris. Envision yourself walking on the Left Bank around the Sorbonne University not too far from the Louvre. This area around the Boulevard St. Michel has myriad shops selling antique prints. All of us have heard stories about how expensive Paris is. Well, it's not true when it comes to old prints. Talk about getting the most for our antiques dollar or in this case our antiques francs. It has to be by purchasing prints. Here we can get something old, of quality, and inexpensive.

A few years ago friends and I spent hours in wonderful print shops in the Latin Quarter. We bought bird prints for about $1.90 each. We didn't even try to negotiate price, a subject we shall get into shortly. The colorful prints came from 1880s French magazines highlighting birds and French landmarks. Back home I bought ready-made frames and took them to my framer for custom-made mats. Over-scaled mats were chosen because that is the way the French do their prints.

One more Paris print story if you are still an unbeliever. As we left the shop of the $1.90 prints, we found another around the corner. This time money was no object. I went all out on these. Guess how much? Before you do, let me tell you they date from about 1760, the era of Louis XV. They came from an architecture book detailing ceiling molding. Would you believe unframed for $5.00 each?

Buy No Hometown Antiques

After Paris, I was fortunate enough to visit two great American antique cities–Charleston, South Carolina and Savannah, Georgia. Having had that pleasant experience with antique prints in France, it seemed like a good idea to buy some depicting these two old havens. While shopping for some of Savannah in Savannah, I accidentally learned a trick about successful antiquing. You see I stumbled upon antique prints of Charleston in Savannah. Seems backwards, doesn't it? If on a budget, never buy antiques in their hometown or state of origin. Chances are everyone appreciates them there which adds more zeros to the left of the decimal point. That means in Ohio, never buy Heisey or Cambridge glass if you expect a bargain. In Boston avoid Grueby Pottery and forget finding early Franciscan Pottery in California shops. That is what hit me when buying

Photograph courtesy of Glenn Hartong.

This 1880s print of Charleston was purchased in Savannah, Georgia. It was less expensive than if it had been purchased in its hometown.

two unframed 1880s prints of Charleston in a fine Savannah shop. Five dollars each was most pleasing, especially when thinking of what shops along King Street in Charleston would ask for comparable ones.

Buy Unframed

If you can, buy your prints unframed and get ready-made frames to save even more money. Always have the mats professionally done because this adds that expensive gallery look.

Trips to Paris or Charleston are not always needed. Sometimes you can find prints with a terrific price already framed in your local antiques mall. I found two English ones dating from 1825 complete with 1940s frames. One illustrates "Eccentrics on High Street in Cheltenham," a fashionable health resort in the early 1800s. The other shows the Pump Room, a tea room in the great antique town of Bath, England. That Neoclassical room looks almost the same today. Neoclassical is a mighty important term that will shortly be explained.

Forty-five dollars was a deal for those two charmers. Just imagine if they had been slightly stained or not a pair, they might have cost even less.

That is enough tips, at least for the time being. We are ready to learn all about antiques. However, one stumbling block that will make speaking fluent antiquese easier must be scrapped. That will be accomplished in the next passage.

No More French

One aspect of antiques that really confuses a lot of people is French terminology and names. Let's clear up our language and it will make learning about antiques painless. It is really very simple.

Loomism: Please stay away from using French terms to describe antiques. (Note: There are a couple of deviations from this *Loomism*–French terms just too divine to avoid.)

"Why not French?" you ask. After all, it is a beautiful language and the Rue de la Paix in Paris certainly sounds ritzier than Peace Street.

But that is the point: Leave French for the French. Or if you wish, benefit from its beauty when dining in a French restaurant or when visiting that glorious country. Let's not use it when talking about our antiques.

Instead, choose easy-to-understand terms to describe our antiques. Forget those intimidating and impossible-to-decipher French expressions such as *fauteuils* when referring to armchairs.

Using English will make it much easier to learn antiquese, which is about to become our second tongue.

Simplicity is the key to mastering antiques.

Consider what happens when French terms are thrown into a novel chosen as a pleasurable pastime to de-stress our lives. We end up feeling stupid. We have no idea of who is doing what

Instead of asking for "bergeres," call them French armchairs.

Photograph courtesy of Skinner, Inc..

to whom and in what type of furnishings. How many times have you been right in the middle of a juicy part and you had to stop and reach for a French-English dictionary to fully understand what was going on? Whether the author has written in a bilingual fashion for atmosphere or to impress, the result is still the same—confusion to readers.

For instance, instead of saying:

"Catherine, wearing a *moire* and *tres decolleté* frock, sat at her *bonheur du jour* sipping her *demitasse*, pondering her next *rendezvous*."

Why not simply say:

"Catherine, in her rather revealing water silk dress, sipped her after-dinner coffee at the writing desk, pondering her next appointment."

Naturally the French version sounds more suggestive. That is due to its justly earned reputation of being the jargon so conducive for romance. That titillating appeal and the fact most

Photograph courtesy of Skinner, Inc..

In Paris this is a commode but in English that term means you-know-what. Call this mid 1700s French piece a chest of drawers.

Photograph courtesy of Skinner, Inc.

By referring to these china closets/curio cabinets by their French term "vitrine," few on this side of the English Channel will understand.

of us have no idea of what is really happening gets our imaginations working overtime. While spicy intrigue can sometimes be fun in novels, we do not need that added difficulty when studying antiques.

What about books on antiques, those megabucks volumes with fancy covers that everyone buys on sale and then puts on the coffee table to show the world he or she has class? The writing style is often so Frenchy and full of pretentiousness that few readers can decipher what the author is attempting to communicate.

Would you be able to translate the following?

"*Avant guarders* of substance quested for *objets d'art* with more *je ne sais pas essence.*"

Why not just get to the point by using simple English? The Loomis approach to writing about antiques is right to the point: highly energetic and without foreplay of flowery words. Here is the Loomis version:

"Rich kooks wanted kinky knickknacks."

Victorians, of course, loved to use French and they are probably the guilty ones for sprinkling French expressions into daily conversations. This habit ultimately led to the controversy.

Photograph courtesy of Skinner, Inc.

The Arc de Triomphe captured by the French artist Andre Gisson (French b. 1910) sounds far more beautiful in French than the English version, "Triumphal Arch." That is the point: leave French to the French and use English terms for our antiques.

Somewhere in the mid-1800s, one of them came up with the pleasant sounding *pie a la mode* for pie and ice cream. And who doesn't love French fries? you might ask. But remember, that is the Americanized version for *pommes frites.*

Collect antique calling cards and leave the *cartes de visites* for Parisians. Small cases that were used as manicure or sewing sets are fun to acquire; but if anyone was to ask for an *etui* anywhere outside of France, the response would probably be "Pardon me?"

After all, if a chest of drawers is called by its French name, *commode,* one might get into trouble. Come to think of it, though, perhaps *pot de chambre* does sound more refined than chamber pot. But no matter into what language it is glitzed, it still serves the same purpose.

P-l-e-a-s-e, no more French!

So when it comes to learning about delightful antiques that add such enchantment to our lives, simplicity is the number one *Loomism. Is It Antique Yet?* will describe and explain everything in easy-to-understand terms chosen to make your self-study course in antiques interesting, enjoyable, educational, and a whole lot easier to follow than a computer manual. Now onward to learning about woods!

5

All About Woods

We need to get right down to the most important ingredient about antiques, which of course is woods. *Is It Antique Yet?* emphasizes furniture because that is the logical and most fun place to embark. Starting with furniture styles is similar to moving to a new place. You learn the area around your home and then branch out to unknown territories. It is the same situation with antiques. When you recognize a chair as Queen Anne, you will see similar trademarks on a silver tea pot. A look as fabulous as those cabriole legs was used on many furnishings.

The lure of wooden antiques is obviously due to the fact that they are made from trees. Not only do forests help our environment organically, but they embellish our lives. Can we even imagine autumn without falling leaves?

"I think I shall never see a poem as lovely as a tree," from that antique poem by Joyce Kilmer sums up the appeal of wood. The only comment to add is: "If a tree had to be cut down, hopefully it was crafted into some terrific antique such as a table or bookcase where its natural beauty still lives."

Sometimes when we see our wooden pieces, whether an ornate plant stand or a spinning wheel, it is hard to envision they all started out as living trees. New furniture clouds our understanding of its origin. Most is made from practically anything including cardboard, plastic, and even once in awhile from genuine wood. Here is another plug for collecting: antique furniture was always made from trees.

Photograph courtesy of Skinner, Inc..

Our wooden antiques started out as living trees such as these captured by American photographer Ansel Adams. (1902-1984)

Has this ever happened to you? In the past I used to just admire the good looks of a wooden antique and tended to overlook that a 1780s oak chair, a pine rocking chair, or a walnut chest of drawers had all once been trees.

Then one day the organic origin of wooden antiques hit me like a ton of logs. A student in my antiques class asked: "What kind of tree grows mahogany?" Like a goof I said, "I don't know." Then I quickly added, "I always thought of mahogany as a chair or table." Well, after we stopped chuckling, I yelled, "Timber, mahogany trees grow mahogany!"

The person who takes lumber and crafts it into a table or stool is known as a cabinet maker. That is the title most experts prefer to call them. It is frowned upon to label them as furniture makers. Who knows the reason? One charming theory is that the term "cabinet maker" comes directly from the French word *ébeniste*. We all know how anything French sounds ritzier; or maybe "cabinet maker" commands more stature. It is something like how one is an attorney rather than a lawyer. Perhaps the furniture legend, Thomas Chippendale, started the expression in the mid-1700s when he was making his masterpieces on St. Martin's Lane in London. Can't you hear him saying to King

George III, "Your Majesty, please refer to me as a cabinet maker, not a furniture maker. After all, I don't make pieces for the riff raff, you know." Anyway, it makes for a nice story.

Excuse the detour, but humorous anecdotes make learning about antiques more fun.

The Big Three

There are six woods that are the most important and appreciatively the easiest to recognize. They will make a good foundation for knowledge about woods. The two auburns are mahogany and cherry; three blondes are oak, maple, and pine; and one brunette is walnut.

MAHOGANY

Just like their names, the auburns tend to be reddish brown, similar to the color of cordovan shoe polish.

The most famous is mahogany. Its first heyday was in the mid-1700s to the mid-1800s. Not grown in Britain or in the American colonies, it had to be imported from the West Indies and Central America. Thus it was expensive and only used for top-of-the-line furniture.

Mahogany has a sedate-looking grain, and in its natural, unfinished state, is the color of rose wine. It is literally quite heavy and dense. It could be carved with minute detail creating very realistic, almost three-dimensional carving. Roses carved into the back horizontal pieces of 1850s chairs and sofas are a good example.

Mahogany's traits also helped end the popularity of other woods for furniture construction. Its heaviness and density, unlike oak and walnut, made mahogany resistant to beetle tunnels. Those have been incorrectly but so charmingly called

Photograph courtesy of Card of Wood, Inc.

Mahogany in its natural state is the color of rose wine.

Photograph courtesy of Skinner, Inc.

Mahogany was used in the 1700s mainly for city-made pieces such as this Chippendale style mahogany chest of drawers.

worm holes. Oak or walnut furniture dating from the 1600s or before often had beetle tunnels.

Around 1750 mahogany became very chic for the rich and famous in London and in New York, Boston or Charleston on this side of the Atlantic. The French were not as crazy about mahogany as the Brits. They preferred other woods and also liked white lacquer and gilding on their furniture.

Mahogany became known as the "aristocrat" of woods. It earned this nickname because when expensive furniture was crafted in England or the United States, it was usually from mahogany. A cabinet maker would not make a kitchen chair from mahogany but rather a sitting room one befitting a Duchess.

After the first Age of Mahogany, it had a second wave from about 1910 to the 1940s. Pieces that date from then are called semi-antiques and follow those 1700s designs. That means there must be a bundle of antique mahogany furniture available for us whether 1700s ones or 1930s semi-antique pieces.

Our antiques idol, Thomas Chippendale, preferred this wood for his 1700s creations. Mr. Chippendale carved fine detailing into his furniture such as carved ball and claw feet on table and chair legs. Chairs of the 1930s were often crafted in the manner of that genius which is a polite way of saying it is a copy of Mr. C's work. This is another plug for getting more antiques dash for our cash by choosing a semi-antique. It is so well-made that we still get the look of fine carving following Chippendale's trademark. The newer piece is done by machinery rather than by hand. Sometimes it is hard to tell the genuine from the later rendition.

Today antique (as well as new) mahogany furniture still gets ritzy status. An antique mahogany piece will usually cost around fifty percent more than a similar one in oak, walnut, or other woods.

CHERRY

Our second auburn, cherry, is probably the most beloved wood. Grown practically everywhere in America, it was mainly used in country pieces. It may have had a humble origin, but today cherry has much clout and gives mahogany a run for those antiques bucks.

Cherry in its natural condition resembles mahogany. This wood is somewhat paler than rose wine, more like a blush. It is particularly strong and close grained which made it popular among American cabinet makers.

Although its pinkish hue is the key to its popularity, cherry has another remarkable trait. Often overlooked is its flamboyant lightning streak of a pale, almost champagne-colored grain. The lighter color can run dramatically through the darker part. Cherry's vivid mixing of these hues adds beauty to any article. We can find good examples in American country pieces, such as sewing tables dating from the early 1800s used today as nightstands.

Together cherry and mahogany have graced many sideboards or chests. It is time to set the record straight about veneer. This term has been misunderstood as an indication of cheapness. This is a time-consuming and skillful process of putting a

Photograph courtesy of Card of Wood, Inc.

Cherry fresh from the forest resembles mahogany with a similar pinkish color.

Photograph courtesy of Skinner, Inc.

Country craftsmen in the mid 1700s made cherry Queen Anne style curvy/cabriole legs like the ones on this table.

very thin layer of a more expensive wood like mahogany over a less expensive one such as pine. A veneered piece is usually top-drawer because much skill and extra effort go into gluing those thin pieces of costlier mahogany over thicker, less inexpensive (but still wonderful) pine ones to make it appear all mahogany. Almost anyone can nail some boards together to make a stool, but how many can veneer?

Regard it as an art that separates the cabinet makers from the furniture makers.

Looking inside a drawer from an 1830s chest of drawers clearly shows how veneering is done. By outward appearances its drawer's facade seems totally created from mahogany. Looking closely at its interior, we see pine on its sides and bottom. Most pieces were made from different types of woods. Not only does this chest of drawers contain mahogany and pine, but it also has cherry. Where do you think? Because the two auburns are so similar in color, cabinet makers would use locally grown cherry for its sides. The two outside end panels were made from cherry to match the hue of the mahogany-veneered drawer fronts. Due to the veneering process only our socks view the pine while the world sees the mahogany facade and cherry sides. It all blended perfectly well together. The best way to describe this piece is by saying, "Mahogany is the primary wood, and pine and cherry are the secondary ones."

Artisans cleverly had to pick a piece of cherry that did not have any pale graining because that would contrast too wildly with the sedate mahogany. Affordable cherry, always so cherished, earned the lovely nickname "the poor man's mahogany."

Cherry may once have been for the budget minded, but unfortunately for us that is no longer true. A cherry candlestick stand can often cost as much as a comparable mahogany one. Just a glance at anything cherry with its uplifting crimson glow makes it worth the extravagance.

OAK

Now on to the blonde woods. These have a color similar to beer. Perhaps the most famous is oak that grows chiefly in north temperate zones and Polynesia. It is quite durable and has been used in construction of houses, ships, and also furniture. Of all the woods, oak is the most honest in the sense that it is the easiest for us to recognize. It has a lively graining. It comes in several hues ranging from those similar to Chablis wine to the robust color of beer.

Oak, along with walnut, was the chief wood for European furniture before the 1700s. Then, as we know, when mahogany became chic, it, as well as walnut, fell from favor. English oak furniture tends to be darker than lighter American oak pieces. This is due to the climatic differences between the two areas.

Have you ever heard that charming expression "golden oak"? The term usually refers to oak furniture such as round dining tables with claw feet made around 1900. As the finish on your great-grandma's table aged, it acquired a lovely, deeper amber color resulting in golden oak. That description has to do with patina. That means the build-up of wax, dirt, fading, and perhaps a few nicks and scratches done by pets. It is something

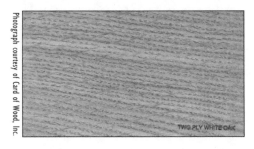

Photograph courtesy of Card of Wood, Inc.

The most famous of the blond woods is oak because it is the easiest to recognize thanks to its "beer" color.

Photograph courtesy of Skinner, Inc.

Kitchen dressers or cupboards like this 1780s English one were made of oak because it was strong and relatively inexpensive.

to treasure because it is what makes an old piece look antique. Bad refinishing can destroy patina. It is so treasured that reproductions can be factory banged to get that worn look. These golden oak mass-produced circa 1900-1910 pieces have really helped make oak popular today among antiquers.

The easiest way to learn more about golden oak is to read the reproduction catalogues of Sears and Roebuck or Montgomery Ward. Around 1900 both stores sold moderately priced china closets with glass on three sides and center post dining tables with claw feet. In 1897 Sears illustrated an oak hall tree/stand complete with built-in bench, hooks, and mirrored section for $7.50. If you found one today in a shop, at least two zeros or probably more would have to be added to that 1897 price.

My antiquer aunt collected 1900 golden oak before it became fashionable as an antique. Aunt Panny got oak goodies for peanuts because they were still considered garage sale stuff. In the 1960s she paid about $25 at a farm auction for a 1910 oak desk. Once in the domestic beer price range, oak pieces have graduated to the price level of imported lager beers. Today her desk would probably sell in a shop for at least $800. Antiquers cannot seem to get enough of golden oak pieces, probably the most sought-after of all antique furniture.

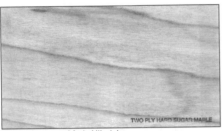

TWO PLY HARD SUGAR MAPLE

Photograph courtesy of Card of Wood, Inc.

Maple's color is similar to oak but its graining is harder to spot.

MAPLE

Another wood that has made a comeback is maple. Maple trees grown the world over are known for their beautiful foliage and in Vermont for their sweet syrup. The grain of maple is so fine it is often hard to see. However, the wood is so strong it is almost impossible to carve. Its natural color ranges from off-white to a light golden tone. Maple ladder back chairs from the mid-1800s give us a good idea of maple's color and grain.

Maple is so strong it was often used for structural parts of furniture requiring strength such as chair legs. The seats were thankfully from softer pine. Cutting boards were made from maple, which is how butcher block furniture got its name.

In America, maple was mainly crafted into country furniture from around the American Revolution until the mid-1800s. The knotty part of the maple tree was cut into thin strips of veneer.

Photograph courtesy of Skinner, Inc.

The strips were often put on drawer fronts of 1840s secretary desks. It added a little oomph to calmer-looking mahogany and cherry seen on the outside of the piece.

Maple furniture has become extremely popular with collectors. A 1700s maple table may sell at auction for double what a comparable cherry or even a mahogany one would fetch.

This Queen Anne maple highboy from Massachusetts dates from 1760.

Photograph courtesy Peter Clark of Somerset House.

(Top) The graining of bird's eye maple is easy to spot due to its lively circular design. (Right) The bird's eye maple on the drawer front of this small work/sewing table from the early 1800s really gives it pizzazz.

Photograph courtesy of Skinner, Inc.

PINE

The next blonde wood is a favorite because antiques made from it are more affordable than in other woods. If that is not reason enough, there is one more great thing about this wood that surely will please you. We will get into that shortly.

Wonderful pine has made a comeback, or should we say, it has finally come into its own. Pine grows all over Europe and North America. The pale grain has slight veins in it. The wood has a lovely soft feeling, as if almost bendable.

Relatively inexpensive, compared to imported mahogany, pine was grown all over the United States. Throughout history it has gotten a bum rap. So pine, lightweight and easy to work, became covered with veneer, hidden in the interiors of drawers or used as painted wall paneling. It even has been painted with a graining effect to look like swankier mahogany or oak.

Once considered the blue plate special of woods, pine has now graduated into nattiness. Think of it as the spaghetti of

Photograph courtesy of Card of Wood, Inc.

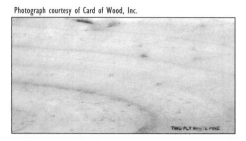

TWO PLY WHITE PINE

Lightweight looking and pale-colored pine does not show dust.

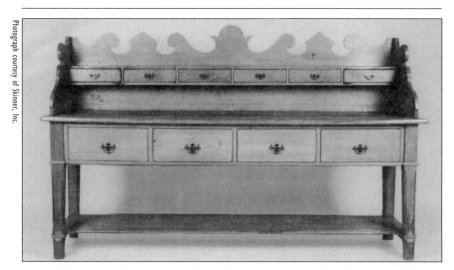

Photograph courtesy of Skinner, Inc.

Pine often got painted which may have happened to this Irish server dating from the early 1800s.

woods. Pine antiques such as washstands were considered only worthy for the kitchen or spare bedroom. Only a mahogany one would do for the master bedroom. Now all that has changed, and pine is very much in vogue. Its new status is similar to how that old blue plate special, spaghetti, has become very chic. Of course, now, it is called pasta. Aren't we glad that pine is still called pine?

Even though pine is still called by its original name, almost everything else associated with it has changed. It has been rediscovered. It is seen in upscale living or dining rooms rather than being hidden in a corner of the kitchen. As maple, cherry, and mahogany antiques have become high-ticket items, pine still has downright friendlier prices.

Pine cupboards show the appeal of this wonderful wood. They were originally made to hold dishes and linens in the kitchen. Today, they may hold the family china, but it is the best set—such as Wedgwood or Minton. Now it stands regally in the dining or family room. It has even become high-tech by hiding the television or VCR behind its doors.

Antique pine furniture is delightful because it is affordable, and its neutral color goes terrifically with other woods. That is a good point to mention: do not be afraid to mix your

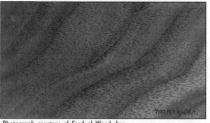

The open grain of walnut and its various shades of brown make it quite adaptable to many styles.

Photograph courtesy of Card of Wood, Inc.

furniture pieces that are made from various woods. Our ancestors did just that.

Speaking of ancestors, my favorite, Gram, best described the appeal of pine: "It does not show the dust like darker woods."

WALNUT

Our next wood is walnut. The brunette does show the dust, but, oh well, we can't have everything. It's not untrue to say that most of us love walnut. Its hues, like chocolate fudge, can range from light to dark. It looks beautiful in any room in any style and with any other wood.

Walnut grows the world over, is durable, and has a some-

Photograph courtesy of Skinner, Inc.

what open, porous grain. This has made it highly desirable for furniture and gun stocks. Walnut, after oak, was the second favorite wood for European furniture before mahogany ruled. A lot of American country pieces were crafted from walnut, such as chests of drawers, tables, and beds.

This magnificent Chippendale style chest on chest from the late 1700s really displays walnut's grain.

Why has walnut enjoyed an almost nonstop popularity? Like a navy blue blazer, it's not showy but certainly in good taste in any setting and in any century.

Wood Stains

While we are learning about woods, there are a few more little things that need to be clarified. Elaborating about the color of woods–the auburns, the blondes, and the brunette–cannot help reminding us about wood stains. Stain is like a watered-down paint that is applied to one wood trying to duplicate the color and look of another. Pine is very good for staining because its porous graining soaks up the stain almost like a sponge.

The practice became common in the late 1800s when most furniture began to be mass-produced. Factories wanted the exposed parts to appear as if they were constructed out of one wood. Sometimes it is hard to determine what a certain wood is because it is buried under stain.

An antique chair is constructed from various woods because each one offers certain advantages. Seats are often pine because its softness made it easier to shape and more comfortable as a seat. Chair legs were often maple or oak for strength. All the parts were painted one color, such as a deep green, or were stained a medium brown to resemble walnut.

Staining wood only changed the various colors but offered no protection. After the stain dried, a varnish was applied which was a solution of resins of alcohol or linseed oil. It was used by cabinet makers to create a shiny, transparent, hard coat to protect the wood's surface.

The problem with staining is that it really did not match the woods it was trying to duplicate. Mahogany stain tended to be so red it resembled iodine; maple somehow became very orangey; cherry a garish pink; and oak a way-too-dark brown. Only walnut somehow escaped the staining method. That was probably because it is the "blue blazer" of woods. Do not worry about those fake colors. In time you will be able to recognize the woods buried under those artificially tinted hues.

Keep a picture in your mind of walnut, cherry, maple, pine,

and mahogany in their unstained condition. Remember them as the big three: blondes, auburns, and brunette.

That's our foundation of woods. Another way to know woods better is to caress wooden pieces. Rub your hands over the top of a cherry worktable to get the lay of the grain. It is too bad so many museums rope off their furniture not allowing us to touch an armrest or table top. It is natural to want to caress a piece of furniture. This helps us to get more familiar with the various woods. Touching them is the sensual approach to antiques. Doing that makes them a beloved antique rather than an unfamiliar old piece of furniture.

So there we have it. Now we can identify the main woods. That will be helpful as we go antiquing and discover more about antiques.

If you want to get more familar with woods, you might acquire my video, "All about Woods," tape II of the *Is It Antique Yet?* series. It has great color shots of the woods discussed here.

Remember what Mr. Kilmer says, "There is never a poem as lovely as a tree." We antiquers want to add one more line, "Except when it has been made into an antique like our great-uncle's maple table."

What is Your Antiques Personality?

Here is a quick point about antiques that will prove useful as we master the great furniture styles.

Have you ever wondered what is your antiques personality?

It does not matter whether a Civil War rifle or a Shirley Temple blue glass mug is your antique cup of tea. We collectors tend to follow two very diverse decorating trails. The first is the uncluttered look, the Georgian, and the second is the opposite, the Victorian.

To figure out your preference, answer this question: Do your china closet shelves have evenly spaced plates and tea cups and saucers? Or, now be honest, are they crammed onto its shelves?

If your answer is that your china is neatly arranged, chances are you prefer the more organized, understated feeling from the Georgian era. Or, if you responded that your hutch is crammed with lots of teacups and saucers and other things, then you are definitely a Victorian type collector.

Here is a closer inspection of these two different outlooks concerning how we decorate our homes with antiques. Both tastes are named after British monarchs. In America we have tended to follow more closely what was fashionable in London before turning our aesthetic eyes to France and other countries.

The first group, Georgian, is named after the four George Hanovers who ruled England from 1714 to 1830. Georgian furniture, silver, china, and other home items came in assorted

Photograph courtesy of Skinner, Inc.

Here is another easy quiz to decide about your antiques personality. Note the chest to the left and the one on the adjacent page. Both chests are English, Chippendale styles and date from the late 1700s.

This chest is practically the way it was when it was brand new.

styles. Compared to the furnishings of the next era, they seem rather staid and sometimes downright plain.

The second taste, Victorian, is in homage to Victoria, the queen who ruled Great Britain from 1837-1901. The items made during her long reign are labeled Victorian.

In order to get a visual impact of the two diverse philosophies, let's think about the movie "Gone With the Wind." Watching a movie for its plot is not as fun as checking out its antiques. "GWTW" warrants twenty viewings! This 1939 classic remains the all-time best movie for antiques because it showcases both Georgian and Victorian decorating. We get to see what was popular before the Civil War and what became the last word in refinement after 1865.

Tara appeals to the Georgian collectors.

Tara, the pre-Civil War home of Scarlett O' Hara, represents Georgian tastes. The furnishings are low-key and sparse. Tara follows the balanced Georgian rule. Any mantel at Tara would have something like this: one perfectly centered picture on the wall above it; below on the mantel's top would be a clock

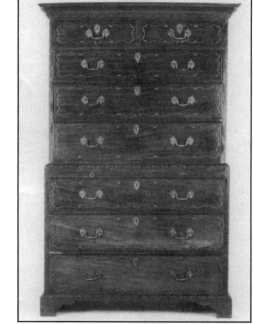

This chest was "jazzed up" a bit during the Victorian age by carving around its side.

If you prefer the one on the left, you are a pre-1840s type collector, if you chose the one on the right, then you are a true Victorian at heart.

Photograph courtesy of Skinner, Inc.

or a china bowl flanked on either side by a pair of vases or candlesticks. That is all. Furniture was usually arranged in the same manner. On either side of the fireplace would possibly be a pair of chairs. Understatement and balance rule.

Just about the time of the War between the States, decorating tastes changed dramatically. Most goods for homes whether chairs or teapots were machine made instead of the slower and costlier handmade production. These were prosperous times, and middle-class households greatly increased. All this abundance made furnishings more plentiful, less expensive, and increased clutter.

Scarlett's Atlanta mansion built after the War follows such trendsetters as Mary Todd Lincoln, Queen Victoria, and the French Empress Eugenie. These women followed the twenty picture rule: "Why put just one framed photo on a table when you can squeeze in nineteen more?" And the fancier the frames the better!

Scarlett's house in Atlanta gave those famous ladies elaborate competition. No more understatement for Scarlett. She wanted to show the world her wealth through her belongings. Clutter was at an all time high!

To get a quick visual impact of Victorian tastes, check one of Scarlett's Atlanta fireplaces. It is as if the Georgian rule never existed. Mantels were regarded as a curio cabinets. Spread across the lace doily were as many vases, photos, and candlesticks that could be shoved onto that narrow space.

The furnishings seen at Tara and the Peachtree Mansion show two widely different decorating principles. Whether Georgian or Victorian, they are both in good or in bad taste depending upon one's view. Remember "clutter is in the eye of the beholder," as Miss Scarlett, Mrs. Lincoln, the Empress Eugenie, and Queen Victoria would agree.

Photograph courtesy of Skinner, Inc.

This painting of Paris by Frank Edwin Scott (American 1862-1929) "St. German des Pres" captures the beauty of this very ancient church and the city that has set so many trends in the world of antiques.

7

A Tale of Two Antique/Antiques Cities

In the world of antiques there are many great nations, China, Italy, Holland, and others just to mention a few. To become intimate with antiques in the most efficient manner possible, we shall concentrate upon France and Great Britain.

A unique relationship between these two has existed since the days of William the Conqueror (1027-1087). History books tell us that Bill, born in France, won the battle at Hastings in 1066, and went on to become the King of England. Sadly, as a result of that struggle, these two nations have not been the best of pals. There have been many wars and few peaceful times. However, that did not stop the movement of designs in clothing, art, food, and furnishings from Paris to London.

As you read this book, it is clear that Charles Dickens wrote it best. Regard our antiques learning as "a Tale of Two Cities." Here is the often repeated antiques story. The French would borrow, or sometimes reinterpret, a design from another country. Then the Brits would copy them. The English variation would probably be less ornate.

Starting in the mid-1700s, "A Tale of Two Cities" would have a bigger title by adding "...and America, too." This meant that a third interpretation emerged–the Yankee version. This could be an American facsimile of the English copying the French or the Americans directly imitating the

Photograph courtesy of Skinner, Inc.

The Canadian artist Frederick Bell-Smith (1846-1923) in his work: "The Clock Tower Westminster from St. George Street," recreates London's Famous landmark. Antiquers owe so much to this city that has brought us everything from Chippendale furniture to Royal Doulton China.

French. All this will become as clear as the crystal in your grandmother's favorite water goblets as you read future chapters.

Finally, these two smashing nations are now good buddies, witness the recent tunnel constructed under the English Channel. We owe this liaison, which always existed artistically but rarely politically, to three rulers. Queen Victoria of Britain, Napoleon III, and the Empress Eugenie of France started the "Good Neighbor Policy" in the mid-1800s. Later when we look at Rococo Revival we shall discover how influential those three were on home decor.

Before Modern Antiques

My flapper grandmother finally realized that yours truly was an incurable antiques addict when she helped me furnish my first apartment. Not terribly pleased, she cried that familiar myth about antiques: "They're not even comfortable." Many people visualize antiques as heavy, dark, and stiff. If you are afraid to use them for fear of turning your house into a mausoleum, you are half right!

Photograph courtesy of Skinner, Inc.

These 1950s English china figurines depict three important members of the royal Tudor family, Henry VIII, his beheaded second wife, Anne Boleyn, and his daughter, Elizabeth I. Tudor-style furniture named in their honor was spooky and as uncomfortable as their ponderous clothing.

Photograph courtesy of Skinner, Inc.

This painted oak cupboard from the late 1600s shows how pre-1710 antiques were downright intimidating and "user unfriendly." Opening those heavy doors required much strength.

To understand how that unjustified rumor was started, visit a museum. Glance at the portraits that date before 1700. Rarely is there a smile or a tranquil pose among those courtly people captured on canvas. No wonder because those wretched-looking people had terribly rigid furniture.

Photograph courtesy of Skinner, Inc.

Another version of a cupboard captures that spooky look common for furniture before the Queen Anne style.

Photograph courtesy of Skinner, Inc.

These chairs explain it all. Who would want to sit in one of these, when more comfortable seating equipment was about to be invented? The left and far right from the late 1600s were named "Cromwellian" after Oliver Cromwell (1599-1658). Rigid chairs such as this helped preserve Puritanism in England. The center European chair looks almost painful.

Those dismal portraits probably hang in pre-1700s room settings. Those funereal decors with all that dark woodwork and ornately carved and bulky furniture, may make you feel like a prisoner in Dracula's castle. Body aches caused by downright hostile furnishings must have caused that count's nastiness.

By sitting in a church pew you experience posteriorly our ancestors' stodgy predicaments. Those who regard antiques as uncomfortable are correct, provided you are referring to pre-1710 ones or to some from the mid-1800s. That is probably how this misconception was started. We are about to meet a style, although almost three hundred years old, that is still considered comfortable and fetching, even by nonantiquers.

Before investigating that bright style, a peep into British history is revealing. How could Tudor-style furniture (1485-1603) exalting spirited Henry VIII (1491-1547) who beheaded two of six wives, be anything but dismal? What shadows must linger around those huge Tudor-style beds with big bulbous rounded carving and wooden canopies? Hank's elder daughter,

Photograph courtesy of Skinner, Inc.

These chairs from around 1730s-1760s when compared to the three previous chairs explains the non-stop adoration of the Queen Anne style: comfort and understated elegance.

Queen Mary (1516-1556), remains known as "Bloody Mary" for her numerous executions. In the late 1500s, as Henry VIII's second daughter, Elizabeth I (1533-1603) ruled, the British stopped Spain from conquering England. "The Virgin Queen" held court while sitting upon rigid chairs with tiny seats and spooky carving. With such unromantic and ghostly furnishings, it must have been rather crafty for Elizabeth not to fulfill her nickname.

The next generation of furniture was Jacobean (1603-1688), named after the Stuart monarchs who ruled after the first Liz. This style was really no better because it still made palaces seem like tombs. Chairs had narrow seats and stiff backs. Decoration on furniture remained ponderous and unhappy.

Around 1688 furniture began to change. In that year King William and Queen Mary started their rule that lasted until

1702. The William and Mary style named in their honor should be given much applause. Its designs became less ornate than earlier styles. This streamlining of decoration would ultimately lead to the Queen Anne style. The tubby bulbous legs seen on 1500s and 1600s pieces, grew lighter. Their shapes became like stacked wooden spools of thread. Sometimes legs would be shaped in a manner that resembled ice cream cones.

Loomism: Furniture made before 1710—so gloomy and ornately carved—looks threatening. The cozy and comfortable next style is the true beginning of modern furniture.

So enough of cramped and terrifying furniture! The next chapter begins our foundation of the great furniture styles that are still universally adored to this day.

The Queen Anne Style

We are now starting our mastery of furniture. *Is It Antique Yet?* emphasizes furniture because it is the most logical, least tricky, and best of all, the most pleasing to uncover. Once you grasp the various designs and dates, you can catch similar traits in other antiques whether silver teapots, china patterns, or even picture frames.

Melancholy carving with its back-and-rump-breaking designs ended during the days of Queen Anne (1665-1714) who ruled Great Britain from 1702 to 1714. Her greatest political accomplishment was the unification of Scotland and England into Great Britain. When this lady's name was given to a style that evolved during her rule, it made her an antiques legend. Today Queen Anne is more famous than most of her fellow rulers (male or female), thanks to this enduring style.

Photograph courtesy of Skinner, Inc.

This 1700s Yankee version of the Queen Anne chair clearly displays the fiddle shaped back which is slightly curved. This ended the rigid feeling of being seated in a church pew. Also the seat is wider and deeper than previous generations of chairs.

This chair from the early 1700s without its seat makes it easy to see its curved back which was started in the Queen Anne era.

Photograph courtesy of Skinner, Inc.

What better starting place for our furniture know-how! The Queen Anne style is more than a trend. It is an emotion and the standard of grace, beauty, and proportion. It is a timeless style. Queen Anne is antiques perfection: the eternal star as other antiques come and go in popularity. Pardon my gusto, but most antiquers would probably agree. It is like that other incomparable luminary, Katharine Hepburn. As other movie stars rise and fall, Miss Hepburn with four Oscars and more than sixty years as a leading lady, will always be revered as she is today. The Queen Anne style, the Katharine Hepburn of antiques, is the grande dame—always adaptable, fashionable, timeless, and like the great Kate, universally adored.

Remember Gram's statement about antiques being uncomfortable? Are you wondering how an almost 300-year-old style qualifies as comfortable and perhaps even modern? Those glum 1600s' paintings glimpsed in a museum illustrate how people perched treacherously upon chairs with unbending backs and small seats. That was downright painful!

Sometime during Queen Anne's reign, an ingenious cabinet maker invented modern furniture. He did this by changing the shape of a chair's back from being almost perpendicular to the seat to being slightly rounded. He devised a chair back, called splat, which repeated the curve of our spines. In the early 1700s a curvy or "spoon" back in the shape of vase or fiddle, called fiddlebacks, was the height of comfort for wooden chairs. Comfort had finally been achieved.

The cabinet maker, besides acting as a decorator, was also a confidant, something like an amateur psychologist to 1700s aristocratic ladies. Probably some duchess complained, "Well, those new chair backs are divine, Darling, but can't you do something about those paltry seats?" Along with spoon backs, a responsive craftsman widened the seat into a more commodious horseshoe shape.

The all-upholstered wing chair achieved total comfort and naturally became known as an easy chair. Used mostly in bedrooms, its wings protected one's head from drafts. Some things never change, such as expensive heat. The height of practical luxury in the mid-1700s was a built-in potty under the chair's cushion. Sequestering the chamber pot there kept its rim from getting too chilly during the winter. With those wider seats and chamber pots hidden under cushions, this style certainly earned its reputation for kindness to humans! Many an American furniture manufacturer has created reproductions (minus that ceramic extra) of the matchless Queen Anne wing chairs. Perhaps you are relaxing in a modern rendition as you read this book.

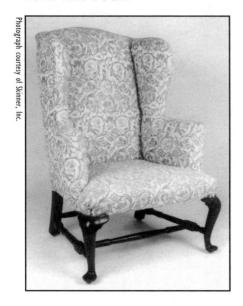

Photograph courtesy of Skinner, Inc.

The Queen Anne style wing chair such as this splendid 1760s model is perhaps the all-time most favorite chair.

Queen Anne Trademarks

An important design trademark of the Queen Anne style is the lack of carving. A scant amount of carving created a soothing, uncluttered feeling making this style ever-contemporary. There were no more fat legs with central bulbs and spooky carving of evil-looking angels. Simplicity is the time-tested ingredient of its durability.

The Queen Anne cabinet maker had other tricks besides little carving and comfortable chairs in his tool box to make these designs so appealing. He used the then little-appreciated, lighter-colored walnut. Oak was no longer fashionable.

Walnut, without past associations of gloomy interiors, is a middle-of-the-road wood as described earlier. While not flamboyant, walnut is always adaptable and serviceable, just like a navy blue blazer.

Photograph courtesy of Skinner, Inc.

This lowboy was crafted from the favorite wood of the Queen Anne era, walnut. This 1760s piece captures the trademarks of the early Queen Anne Style: cabriole legs, little carving except for the incised/concave fan carving in the bottom center drawer, and that very delicate look.

The French version of the cabriole leg is on this Louis XV style walnut table from the mid 1700s.

Photograph courtesy of Skinner, Inc.

Another dead giveaway clue of the Queen Anne style is that it has bowlegs called cabriole. Here is that one French term, fellow antiquers, that is too wonderful to toss aside. All it means is "goat." It does sound more pleasing to say a Queen Anne chair with cabriole rather than goat legs. I hope you understand this one foreign word exception because the French justly win the contest for this one.

The rounded cabriole leg repeated the wavy, curved look of the chair's back. The technical description of a cabriole leg is a knee-leg and concave (rounded) ankle. Besides cabriole legs, you can spot this curviness in the spoon back, aprons (the horizontal front piece between the legs) of chairs, and the single or double curved fronts of chest of drawers.

The trendy French started using the cabriole leg in the late 1600s, changing the spelling from the Spanish *capra* meaning goat. About the same time, the Dutch started crafting chairs with cabriole legs. Perhaps when William and his wife Mary left their native Netherlands to become rulers of England, they brought some chairs with cabriole legs. Horizontal bracers between legs were used to strengthen the early, skinnier cabriole legs.

By the late 1720s, the cabriole leg grew stouter and stronger, no longer needing stretchers. Usually only the front legs of a chair were curved and the back ones were straight for strength. Once in a while you may see a country Queen Anne piece with rounded legs instead of cabriole. They only hint at being slightly cabriole by a little bow to their shape. The cabinet maker made a less expensive version by turning them on a lathe. They are still charming, and pieces with this type of legs are less dear to buy.

Photograph courtesy of Skinner, Inc.

A rurally made maple tea table from the 1700s has no cabriole legs, instead has rounded ones turned on a lathe. These were less expensive to make, and it has pad feet.

The British artist William Hogarth (1697-1764), known for his engravings that spoofed British society, praised cabriole legs. In his written work, *Analysis of Beauty* (1753), he said that "The cabriole leg is adding grace to beauty." His sensitive appraisal resulted in "fiddleback" chairs also being called "Hogarth" chairs. A charming way to immortality for celebrated people was to have a chair named after them. It has undoubtedly helped keep the stature of Martha Washington vigorous throughout time by having a chair christened in her honor.

Early Queen Anne cabriole legs ended in a simple pad foot also called a duck foot because that is exactly what it resembles. The pad foot was replaced by a more ornate one coming from

Photograph courtesy of Skinner, Inc.

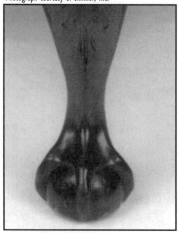

Oriental designs. England started trading in the Canton region of China in 1635. By Anne's day, the British yearned for anything Chinese. Blue and white porcelain, silk, tea, and other goodies were

A ball and claw foot, this design symbolized a dragon's paw holding the pearl of wisdom.

Although this games table from the early 1700s is Dutch, it could easily pass as Queen Anne style. Made from walnut, having cabriole legs with carving on the knees, and those ball and claw feet make it hard to believe that it is not English.

Photograph courtesy of Skinner, Inc.

imported to England. These delicacies delighted Anne's court much the same way discoveries from space explorations will entice future generations.

Trying to cash in on the Chinese frenzy in the hopes of selling more furniture, a London cabinet maker copied the Chinese ball and claw foot replacing the pad foot. This design symbolized a dragon's paw holding the pearl of wisdom.

The fancier foot set off the yearning for a little more dash to other parts of Queen Anne furniture. The shell motif fit the need perfectly. The carved, rounded shell, looking almost like an advertisement for Shell Oil, added the right amount of curvature and restrained decoration. It was the emblem of the Crusaders who tried to free the Holy Land from the Moslems between the eleventh and thirteenth centuries. This design reemerged around 1720 in the furniture of the French King Louis XV at his palace, Versailles, near Paris. London, ever conscious of Parisian trends, added Rococo shells very cautiously to the knees of cabriole legs, chair aprons, middle drawer fronts, and chair backs. This stingy addition of shells and the ball and claw foot did not detract from the style's ever-welcomed simplicity. No one wanted the gloomy furniture from the past that brought up visions of much bloodshed.

Loomism: Queen Anne style has two "substyles." The reaction to the ornateness of previous centuries caused early Queen Anne style to have no carving, pad feet, and skinny cabriole

Photograph courtesy of Skinner, Inc.

The carved Rococo shells on this chair's back and knees of the cabriole legs date it from the late Queen Anne period of about 1770.

legs. The second used the ball and claw foot and slightly fatter legs with more carving, usually in the form of a shell.

Dividing Queen Anne into two substyles prepares us for grasping the next trend.

It is so sad how all of the children of Queen Anne and Prince George died before reaching adulthood. Those two suffered terribly, but maybe Queen Anne knows this style named in her honor has brought joy and comfort to many generations.

After Queen Anne's death, a new family–the Hanovers–ruled Britain. The first was George I, and that is another antiques story. It is important to know that the Queen Anne style continued to be made both in Britain and America long after her rule. There is never a stop date, when one style ends and another starts. Most slide into each other meaning older designs are being crafted at the same time as the newest.

To understand this "sliding" theory take a look at a Group II Collector. Being very self-assured this person would say to their decorator: "I don't care what the latest color is. I want the same yellow for my living room that my aunt had for thirty years." Just remember, furniture back then was individually custom made and there are no set years for each look. That is

Photographs courtesy of Skinner, Inc.

Here are two versions of the Queen Anne highboy. The first is made from maple dating from 1740-1760. It is often called a flat top. The second in cherry is from about 1770, and is known as a bonnet top. The highboy is so associated with the Queen Anne style, that is hard to believe they were crafted in any other style.

why the word *circa*, meaning approximately, is so useful in guessing an antique's age.

The best way to have the Queen Anne style etched in your scrapbook of styles is to pick three definitive examples. It is easy and most have those delightful cabriole legs.

You may have sat upon a Queen Anne chair the last time you feasted in a dining room. The Queen Anne or Hogarth, in honor of our antiques buddy, Bill, had cabriole legs, a w-i-d-e seat, and a solid central vase or fiddle-shaped splat from the frame of the seat to top of the back.

This is the first modern (i.e., comfortable) piece of furniture because of its rounded back following the curve of our backs. These chairs were first made from walnut. Then around 1750, mahogany became the wood for city pieces. It is hard to believe,

Photograph courtesy of Skinner, Inc.

Another popular chair of the Queen Anne era was the corner or roundabout one such as this 1700s New England walnut and mahogany model.

but sometime around 1780, cabinet makers stopped making Queen Anne chairs in favor of other fashionable styles. Then in the late 1870s, American furniture makers started reproductions of these great pieces. If a reproduction dates from circa 1875 to 1890, it has acquired the charming and exalted sounding name: a Centennial piece. That means it dates from around the time of America's one hundredth anniversary celebration. It was held in Philadelphia and called the Centennial of 1876. It glorified America's freedom from Great Britain and was similar to a world's fair. Today the Queen Anne style is still in full glory with all the reproductions being made and purchased by people who think they do not like antiques. (Ha!)

The highboy is to the Queen Anne style what the Eiffel Tower is to Paris. To tourists, that famous landmark is Paris, just as the highboy is to antiquers the Queen Anne style. Highboys were first created in the late 1600s in the English William and Mary style. Originally they were known as tall boys. It seems the Brits were not too fond of them and in the mid-1700s started preferring chests-on-chests, which is literally one chest of drawers on top of another. Yankee craftsmen perfected the highboy, and they were made as late as the 1790s. Thankfully, reproductions have been made since the 1880s.

The highboy consists of two parts, a chest of drawers above and a stand below with one to three drawers. All this was supported by those shapely cabriole legs. The earliest ones had flat tops and are less expensive than the ones with broken arch pediments and finials. A pediment is like a triangular piece of wood put on top of the chest to jazz it up, and the broken part means it is cut out in the center. Finials are wooden ornaments sometimes resembling an urn that were added to the top. You will find similar versions on 1700s grandfather clocks. Besides being less costly, the flat tops are great for displaying a favorite bowl or figurine.

The lowboy is one of the most graceful and understated pieces of furniture. The term lowboy is a modern nickname for what really should be called a dressing or toilet table. It held a lady's mirror and other paraphernalia. It was introduced shortly after the highboy and was often a companion piece to the highboy. It resembles the bottom of a highboy, usually has three little drawers, and sometimes one long, horizontal one above the three. They are usually rather lightweight looking. Be

Photograph courtesy of Skinner, Inc.

One more look at a "pre-modern" chair in order to appreciate the Queen Anne style.

careful when buying one. Be certain it is a lowboy and not the base of a beheaded highboy. When shopping, always go to a reputable seller. Ask if the piece is a genuine lowboy. Have all the correct information put on your receipt and you will succeed at safe antiquing.

Purchasing Queen Anne furniture can be mind-boggling, especially with all those zeros in the prices. Shop cleverly. Be a Group II Collector and buy less-than-perfect at downright more affordable prices. Choose married pieces for a highboy or those great semi-antiques from the 1920s and onwards.

Our antiques epic continues in the next section about the first true superstar in the world of antiques. Do not worry; he was one smart guy and did not change the Queen Anne style–too much.

10

Thomas Chippendale: The Ralph Lauren of the 1700s

Queen Anne died in 1714 without any heirs. There was much searching to find a new monarch. Finally a distant relative was found. George Louis of Hanover (1660-1727) became George I of Great Britain and ruled from 1714 to 1727. After him came his son, George II (1683-1760) who is the papa of America's final King, George III (1738-1820). The last of the Georges in a row, the IV, was quite a party boy but also loved fine furnishings. The next chapter has some juicy tidbits about his collecting habits.

The combined years of their reigns, 1714 to 1830, are called the Georgian era in their honor. Antiques crafted during their lifetimes are often labeled "Georgian." This expression helps pinpoint an object's age or origin. It explains that it is British and dates from one of their reigns. An item sometimes is categorized by naming a specific George. Calling a chair "George III" sounds mighty classy, but it does not give us any inkling of its style. That can be confusing. Besides, George III did not make or design any furniture because he was too busy trying to keep the American colonies.

Try to avoid, whenever possible, naming an antique after a ruler. It is like naming early horseless carriages by the name of the president in office when the car was manufactured. Thus World War I era cars would be called "Wilson autos." It is more precise to call them by their maker's name, such as Ford. The same is true with furniture styles that date from the mid-1700s.

King George III (1738-1829) of Great Britain who ruled during the heyday of Thomas Chippendale. Through the years English, Chippendale-style furnishings are often called George III. Avoid using a ruler's name when possible to make leaning styles easier. Say: "English, Chippendale style."

Photograph courtesy of Skinner, Inc.

Before then there were few if any famous or identified cabinet makers, so we call a piece by the ruler's name saying a Queen Anne chair. We are about to unravel clearer systems to describe antiques dating from Georgian days.

The Queen Anne style did not end with her death. Besides its understated elegance and comfort, there were several other reasons for its durability. Whether table legs or women's bonnets, fashion, lacking today's blitz media, was slower to change. Also, our modern throw-away attitude did not exist. Something was not cast off just because it was damaged. Socks were darned, and when a table broke, it was fixed. Almost everything was still being crafted by hand. So repairing was less expensive and more efficient than waiting six months for a custom made and expensive replacement.

All this meant that people were not so orientated to keeping up with the latest. A chair or table was not stored in the attic or barn just because it was not the latest from London or New York. Perhaps a Queen Anne side chair would be relegated to the guest room when a new one in the latest model was acquired for the parlor. Wing chairs with that conveniently hidden compartment probably never left most bedrooms until the advent of indoor plumbing.

In the mid-1700s, breakthroughs were being made in furniture. The late Queen Anne style grew stouter and more robust

This Chippendale style wing chair plainly continues the design of the late Queen Anne style. Chippendale called this "the English style." Notice the fat cabriole legs and the ball and claw feet. This chair does not have a seat cushion while others did.

Photograph courtesy of Skinner, Inc.

in appearance than delicate-looking earlier versions. From around 1730 onwards, cabriole legs became heavier with shell carving on the knees. The simple pad or duck foot went Chinese and became the ball and claw foot.

As the chapter about woods explained, the introduction of mahogany, replacing oak and walnut for fashionable furniture, made antiques history. It became the wood for the rich and famous. Ball and claw feet, Rococo shells, and other details required a dense wood. Mahogany filled the bill. As you know, unlike oak and walnut, it was resilient to beetle tunnels and could be minutely carved.

A big event in the 1700s concerning antiques happened. Some cabinet makers were establishing their reputations by

A late 1700s side chair with ball and claw feet that first started in the late Queen Anne style and continued by Mr. Chippendale. The stretchers are similar to the ones on earlier chairs. The carved back/splat is pure Chippendale.

signing or attaching a paper label to their creations. This follows the number one rule for success in artistic creation. The artist, silversmith, cabinet maker, or china maker should always clearly mark his or her name on the work. It not only shows confidence but is good business. This way people can recognize the product. That is what happened about this time in Britain and the American colonies. People began identifying certain pieces coming from a specific craftsman. "Oh yes, that chair is by Mr. So and So," was for the first time being heard. Then one name became the most distinguished.

In every generation in any field there is one person whose name is always mentioned way ahead of other contemporary competitors. In English literature it is William Shakespeare. American baseball certainly brings to mind Mickey Mantle. When discussing famous television interviewers, Barbara Walters is probably the best known. The 1700s had its superstars in the area of antiques.

By the late 1750s one cabinet maker had become more famous than all the others. Mr. Thomas Chippendale is beyond a doubt the superstar of English furniture. He was born in Yorkshire around 1718 and as a youth went to London to seek his fortune. In 1753 he opened his shop at #60 St. Martin's Lane, not far from St. Martin's in the Field church. Although no longer standing, a historical marker proclaims it as the site of the master's location.

This gentleman was no great inventor, and he really had no new designs. How did he achieve more than 200 years of nonstop adoration?

Mr. Chippendale, besides being a fine artist, was also a superb business man. He knew the key to success was to publish, and he did, three times! His book, *The Gentleman and Cabinet-Maker's Director* was published in 1754, 1755, and 1762. Other competitors such as Nice and Mayhew published theirs, but Chippendale's was considered the best. It was stylish, well-done, and became the *Gone with the Wind* of its time. It made Chippendale a household name. Guess what else happened? The styles he described have since been given his name. No one

Photograph courtesy of Skinner, Inc.

Although this gilded English mirror dates from the late 1800s, it is in the style know as "Chinese Chippendale."

ever says, "I have a 1700s English Chinese-looking mirror." Rather: "I have a Chinese Chippendale mirror." Mentioning his name says it all: quality, and haughty as it may sound, it also discreetly whispers that hard-to-define essential—gentility.

The Gentleman and Cabinet Maker's Director was like a cookbook with recipes of furniture styles. His first book had one hundred sixty designs for furniture. The third had more than two hundred. Mr. Chippendale explained through his drawings how to construct tables, fire screens, beds, and chairs. Also included were the design trademarks for each style, and here they are:

Chinese Chippendale

In the mid-1700s, England, Europe, and the American colonies were still crazy about anything Chinese. Europeans were also trying to duplicate the fine shell-like porcelain invented by the Chinese. So Chippendale cleverly "borrowed" some of their designs. He used Chinese patterns such as square legs and trellis-looking backs for chairs. These traits are now known as "Chinese Chippendale." He also knew the importance of novelty to keep selling more furnishings. Clothing manufacturers do the same with the ever-changing heights of skirts and widths of ties. He reshaped chair legs from cabriole of Queen Anne to straight. Those were christened "Marlborough" legs.

Photograph courtesy of Skinner, Inc.

Mahogany side chairs such as these follow the style that is known as the Chippendale style. Mr. C. borrowed from the Chinese the square legs and the carved splats in the back of the chairs. The are often called "ladder backs" for obvious reasons.

Along with square-shaped legs, his chair backs had lattice work resembling Chinese pagodas. Even his gilded mirrors duplicated those structures. They had a trellis-type design carved into the frame holding the looking glass. Mr. Chippendale even came up with a bed with a pagoda-shaped canopy.

His perfection of the Chinese tastes was far-reaching. His beautiful effects still embellish our homes all these centuries later. The love of anything Chinese brought about the perfection in the mid-1700s of Chinese-type wallpaper of flowers and birds. This motif has become timeless in its appeal.

Gothic

One of his "recipes" that was the least popular was the Gothic. Chairs had pointed Gothic-shaped arches instead of the better-selling trellis-shaped splats/backs. This repeated the architectural shape of Medieval, Gothic churches. Those edifices have arches everywhere from the pointed tops of stained-glass windows to the vaulted ceilings. This look was perhaps too "spiritual" in feeling for most. Those chairs, whose backs were not at all comfortable, reminded one of a place of worship. That probably limited one's gusto for unholy activities. So people chose other styles.

French Taste/Rococo

When it came to the next style, Mr. Chippendale proved himself as the ultimate "hero" of the "Tale of Two Antiques Cities." Although English, he looked to the Palace of Versailles near Paris for design inspiration. His French taste followed the French Rococo style, or as it is called in France, Louis XV. Its trademark, the cabriole leg, was also used in the earlier Queen Anne style. Remember that both the French and the Brits borrowed that wonderful leg design from the Dutch and Spanish.

The term "Rococo" comes from two French words. Rocaille means rock, and coquille denotes shell. It was popular in France around 1740, and it was this look that Chippendale labeled the French style. Wooden pieces had much carving such as shell designs on aprons, those front horizontal pieces between the tops of legs, and knees of the cabriole legs. The exposed wooden

Photograph courtesy of Skinner, Inc.

This Louis XV/Rococo style sofa is exactly the style that inspired Chippendale's French taste.

frame of a chair was often gilded. Pieces had a curvy undulation such as bow fronts on chests of drawers.

This style was better received than the Gothic. All that frivolous Rococo carving was probably too "highly strung" to appeal to the more restrained tastes of the British and Yankees. That fancy carving was expensive to craft so only the palace crowd could afford it. During the reign of George III's granddaughter, Queen Victoria, a revival of this style became the rage for the Brits and Americans.

The English Style

Mr. Chippendale was certainly smart enough not to mess around too much with the perfect Queen Anne style. He endorsed it by giving it a new name, the English style. Was he ever wise! Continuing the Queen Anne style was his most successful career move.

His English style, although a continuation of the Queen Anne, had a slightly different flourish. As a person gets older, there is a tendency to add weight. That is what happened as the Queen Anne style aged. Younger Queen Anne versions from the 1720 era had skinny cabriole legs and little carving. It was so delicate looking. These designs as crafted by him and other cabinet makers grew stouter and more ornate. Those are the

Photograph courtesy of Skinner, Inc.

Mr. Chippendale's book *The Gentleman and Cabinet-Maker's Director* spread the Chippendale style far and wide. This country version of a Chippendale style chest of drawers dates from 1780s.

A Yankee country version in cherry of a breakfast table or Pembroke table in the manner of Mr. Chippendale.

Photograph courtesy of Skinner, Inc.

lines of what we earlier called the late Queen Anne period. The cabriole legs grew huskier, and ball and claw feet replaced the simpler duck or pad feet.

Side chairs were his most famous design. He continued the basic look of the Hogarth chair. His version was stouter and had added touches that have come to be considered his own ideas. Mr. Chippendale loved carving on furniture, so mahogany certainly became fashionable at the right time for him. He carved splats which before were solid in the shape of a vase or fiddle. Now Mr. Chippendale, or one of his assistants, carved it to resemble a spiraling ribbon. These splats are called ribband/ribbon backs. Vase or fiddle backs of the Queen Anne style became ribband/ribbon backs of Chippendale's English Style.

Mr. Chippendale invented a piece of furniture that reveals his romantic spirit, which was usually overshadowed by his business sense. For couples in the 1700s, eating breakfast in those barn-like dining rooms was sometimes just plain unprovocative. Mr. Chippendale's Pembroke table, was a small version of a dining table. It had a drop leaf on each side of its top and rested upon four straight a la Chinese legs. How this table got its name is a sweet fable. It seems the Duchess of Pembroke, a client of Mr. Chippendale, detested breakfasting in her dining room. She asked him to come up with something smaller for

Photograph courtesy of Skinner, Inc.

In the late 1700s American cabinet makers still made highboys, but the British generally turned to making a later version of highboys, a chest on chest. These literally were a chest of drawers upon another. Yanks did not make too many of these, preferring the highboy. This rare American chest on chest, made of cherry, follows the Chippendale style.

eating breakfast in her boudoir. Who knows if that is true, but it makes a great antiques tale.

Today Pembroke tables, with a central drawer in the Chippendale style, are used as end tables in swanky living rooms.

Mr. Chippendale's book tremendously increased his business and made him a legend in his lifetime. His shop made furniture for the big stars of his day such as David Garrick (1717-1779), the famous Shakespearean actor.

Although there were other successful English furniture makers, he became the number one in antiques history. What he called the English style is now known as the Chippendale. Homes decorated with his mahogany furnishings, mirrors, and Chinese-style wallpaper with floral designs personify what most consider the English look. It is so chic that interior designers are still decorating homes in a decor that is more than two hundred years old. It is as the French say: "it takes at least one hundred years or more to learn what is good art and literature." Good furnishings should be added to that saying.

There was another far-reaching effect of Chippendale's book. Now the cabinet maker in the American colonies whether in Philadelphia, New York, Charleston, or Boston was no

A Chippendale style desk/bookcase in cherry dates from the time of the American Revolution. Its has a pediment top with finials very similar to the "bonnet top" of Queen Anne highboys. The drawer part has a curvy serpentine shape. The feet are another variation of the Chippendale style, ogee. Think of them as compacted cabriole legs. Bases similar to this desk have been reproduced by American factories for over a hundred years. Today they are called by the generic name, "Governor Winthrop desks."

Photograph courtesy of Skinner, Inc.

longer behind the times in furniture. They eagerly bought Chippendale's book. Soon ball and claw feet and ribbon back chairs decorated some sophisticated homes in the colonies. The downside is that this fanfare for his creations undoubtedly ended the Queen Anne style.

If Mr. Chippendale made even one-tenth the furniture that is said to be his, he would still be working at his St. Martin's Lane shop. He probably, at the most, only did a small percentage of what is labeled his. The man may be an antiques god, but he was only human! Provenance, that important word that keeps coming up, has much to do with verifying if a piece is truly by the genius's hand. Harewood House in Yorkshire has accounts dating from 1772 authenticating purchases of Mr. Chippendale's furnishings.

Unlike some artisans, Mr. Chippendale believed that imitation is the sincerest form of flattery. Many American cabinet makers followed his designs. Benjamin Randolph (1721-1791) from Philadelphia made a table following Mr. Chippendale's French Rococo look. When new in 1769, it cost about 94 pounds. That sum had the purchasing power equal to about one-seventh the cost of an elegant city house.

No wonder these antiques sell today in the millions. Group II Collectors know how to get the Chippendale look and quality without big bucks. Antiques malls and shops usually offer wonderful semi-antique reproductions that offer ball and claw feet, ribband/ribbon backs, and other Chippendale designs at affordable prices.

At the height of Chippendale's career, there were some discoveries made in Italy that revolutionized furnishings. That's another style(s) and chapter. We are not yet finished with Mr. Chippendale. Being a good business person, he continued to be adaptable. His story continues, but a look at one of his contemporaries will be enjoyable.

Photograph from author's collection.

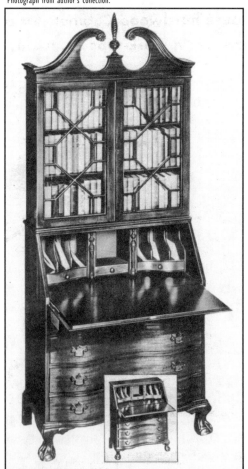

The Chippendale style is enduring. Here is a 1940s version of a Chippendale style secretary desk. Notice the ball and claw feet, broken pediment top, and serpentine front. The desk in the inset is called a "Governor Winthrop" desk.

11

A 1700s Achiever

While Thomas Chippendale was crafting his master-pieces in mahogany, another Englishman was creating wonders from clay. Call him the "Chippendale" of the china industry.

Our gentleman was born in 1730 in the Staffordshire region of mid-central England. This area is known for its English china as Detroit is for American automobiles. The youngest of thirteen children, our antiques legend was born into a poor potter's family. By the time he died in 1795, this 1700s achiever was a millionaire who revolutionized dishes.

Like many in his day, our legend naturally followed his family's footsteps and went into pottery. In those times the industry was still very backwards. Most items were shaped upon the potter's wheel. Wet clay was placed upon a flat disc. To turn it, the artisan pumped a foot pedal attached by an axle to the top round piece. Then it went in a circular direction which helped the potter's hand shape the clay into a vase or whatever.

In the case of our subject, however, there was a glitch. Small pox at age twelve left him with a continuously infected right knee. Without two good knees to operate the potter's wheel, our idol's prospects in the china business seemed unpromising. This device demanded two good legs. This gentleman was at a loss, and like a true achiever he took a negative situation and made it positive.

Photograph courtesy of Skinner, Inc.

The gentleman himself on the right and his beloved business partner, Thomas Bentley on the left, as depicted by Wedgwood's descendants in the early 1800s.

Thank goodness his inventive and creative spirit made him turn his energies away from actually shaping items. Instead he perfected designing and manufacturing china. He, like Mr. Chippendale, had the perfect blending of the artistic along with the important business sense. That terrific combination can lead to immortality in the annals of antiques.

He made quality, inexpensive, and pretty everyday china. No one had done that before him. As a good marketing move he named this line after Queen Charlotte who bought a set. Her husband, King George III, and she dined upon "Queensware."

In 1774 after four years and thousands of experiments, he came up with the famous blue and white Neoclassical Jasperware. Renditions grace museums and collections all over the world, and it is still being crafted today.

He may have been a small-town boy, but he knew London was where to make the big pounds in order to cater to the rich and famous. In August 1768, with the help of his beloved partner, Thomas Bentley, he opened a showroom in the vicinity of Chippendale's London workshop. In order to establish his reputation, he made it a point to sell to all the right people, including a 1,000-piece set to the Empress Catherine of Russia.

The blue and white Neoclassical Jasperware ceramics became a hallmark of Wedgwood.

Not only was he a kind and generous employer, but this gentleman was an activist for human rights. Before it was fashionable to be against slavery, this man was an abolitionist. Some of his Jasperware was crafted with a design depicting a slave asking this poignant question: "Am I not a man and a brother?" That artistic triumph helped end slavery.

Besides all those accomplishments, we Americans revere him for two other special reasons. As early as 1768 this businessman

Jasperware panels even decorate fine furniture such as these English chairs from the late 1800s.

Fine Ceramics
featuring Wedgwood

Auction	Saturday, April 3, 1993 at 10 a.m. in Bolton, Massachusetts	*Bolton Gallery* 357 Main Street Bolton, Massachusetts 01740
Preview	Thursday, April 1, 1993 Friday, April 2, 1993 Saturday, April 3, 1993	2 to 8 p.m. 2 to 8 p.m. 8 to 9:30 a.m.
Sale 1501	Catalogue #1501 available for $18.00, $20.00 by mail, price list included.	

SKINNER, INC.
Auctioneers and
Appraisers of Antiques
and Fine Art

357 Main Street
Bolton, MA 01740
508-779-6241
Fax 508-779-5144

2 Newbury Street
Boston, MA 02116
617-236-1700
Fax 617-247-2903

Front Cover: Lot 332 (Detail)

Wedgwood is definitely the star among ceramics. Just look at this page from Skinner's auction catalogue.

The Wedgwood firm still loves Washington and Yankees. This 1976 bust of our beloved leader was crafted to commemorate the Bicentennial of American Independence.

Photograph courtesy of Skinner, Inc.

had five tons of white clay, the main ingredient for his china, delivered to his factory in England. Guess from where it had been imported? It came from the mountains of western North Carolina near the present town of Highlands. Americans rarely hear stories about our former mother country, Great Britain, buying goods from the American colonies, but our antiques hero did.

Although a loyal British subject to King George III, (how could he be anything else when the queen was his client?) he was discreetly pro-American during the revolution. Ever the good businessman, he thought an independent country would become more prosperous which eventually would increase sales of his china.

Rumor has it he even put his china where his mouth was. He designed commemorative pieces glorifying American statesmen such as that other important George, as in Washington. He had such faith in those "rebels" that pieces were made even before America actually won its independence.

Our legend's renown does not end with his lifetime but extends to other members and generations of this family of achievers. Perhaps you have read the theories of evolution written by his grandson, Charles Darwin? As for the man himself, his designs are still made and copied today.

Quite a series of accomplishments, is it not, for a young boy born into a poor family and afflicted with smallpox at age twelve? (By the way, when he was in his late thirties, he had that bad leg amputated and had a fine wooden one made. Then he went right back to work.)

Whenever china crafted during his reign or by his descendants is mentioned, there is no need to use adjectives to describe its quality, beauty, and timelessness. Just saying his name tells it all.

Ladies and Gentlemen, there is only one "e" in his name, and there is only one . . . Josiah Wedgwood (1730-1795).

P.S. This antiquer could go on forever singing Mr. Wedgwood's praises. If you ever get the chance to visit the Wedgwood factory, near Stoke-on-Trent in England, you will love it. Those wonderful people at Wedgwood continue the master's gentility. Just like their first boss, they really like Americans.

After seeing Wedgwood, take extra time and visit the elegantly understated tomb of Josiah and his beloved wife, Sarah, in the cemetery in Stoke. When yours truly brought them flowers, I asked Mr. Wedgwood's spirit if my puppy could be named Josiah in his honor and if he would consent to becoming the patron saint of antiquers.

12

The "Heppleton" Style

Furniture styles come and go. It is fun to see how historical events can literally change the shape and look of even our chairs and china.

These days the term "Neoclassical" is mighty chic. It is used everywhere from the latest architectural review in the *New York Times* to decorating magazines. The prefix Neo means new, revival, or comeback. Classical refers to the Classical world which consisted mostly of Rome, Greece, and Egypt.

The term Neoclassical was born in the mid1700s. How did this happen? It is a story of ancient times and a famous

Photograph courtesy of Skinner, Inc.

This pair of paintings attributed to Giovanni Paolo Pannini (Italian 1691/2-1765) "Italian Ruins," creates on canvas the Neoclassical style born in the mid 1700s. Notice how columns are an important part of Roman architecture.

Photograph courtesy of Skinner, Inc.

Wedgwood Jasperware plaques from the late 1800s portraying Louis XVI and Marie Antoinette. The Neoclassical style in France is called "Louis XVI."

mountain. About fourteen miles south of Naples, Italy, there was a Roman city of about 15,000 residents. In August 79 A.D., Pompeii and nearby Herculaneum were buried under a shower of ashes and cinders from the volcanic eruption of nearby Mount Vesuvius. Two thousand souls lost their lives in Pompeii. As the volcanic flow dried, it hermetically sealed the buildings and even furnishings.

When Pompeii was accidentally discovered in 1748, excavation began. This was more difficult at Herculaneum because another town had been built over the buried one.

Rome and other cities dating from Classical times still exist, but they have been constantly changed by the inhabitants. Buildings are always being torn down and then new ones constructed. To find a Roman city in such an unaltered state that it was almost brand-new was a first, and it proved a treasure trove.

The discoveries from Pompeii, such as furniture and pottery, created a sensation across Europe and the American colonies. One man in particular helped to create this zest for Classical designs.

About 1732 in England, the Society of Dilettante was started to promote the study of artifacts. The expression "dilettante" comes from this group. It means someone who dabbles in the arts but does not have to worry about money. One of the main objectives of this bunch was to study art. This was accomplished on what came to be called the Grand Tour. It is something like a college student spending a year in a foreign university. This escapade usually included stops at Rome, Venice, Flanders, the Netherlands, and Paris.

After Pompeii was discovered, a Scotsman on the Grand Tour fell in love with the Roman ruins. An architect, Mr. Robert Adam (1728-1792) spent four years in Italy and then published a book of drawings of the ruins. As a result of his popular publication, the Neoclassical style was born.

When we think of Classical times, we envision togas, fig leaves, and athletic-looking people running around in that most antique costume of all, their birthday suits. Put your mind on an antiques level and ponder their architecture. Temples immediately come to mind. The big trademark of those places are columns and symmetry. Those fluted circular vertical supports held up roofs in Classical buildings from bathhouses to palaces. The straight column look is the key to Neoclassical design. Mr. Adam brought that look to Britain and ultimately to the world. The Neoclassical was a smash. China makers, silversmiths, and cabinet makers, including Mr. Chippendale, would follow Mr. Adam's designs.

Remember that Mr. Adam has no "s" in his name. He was an architect and author, not a politician. Those gentlemen with "s" in their names, John, and his son John Quincy, both got to live in America's most famous Neoclassical residence, the White House.

Mr. Adam, like Mr. Chippendale, published a book of designs. *The Works in Architecture* came out in three sections starting in 1773. It had drawings for furniture, as well as residences looking like Roman palaces. Mr. Adam followed Mr. Chippendale's success by writing a book, and Mr. Chippendale, ever the good business man, followed Mr. Adam's achievement by crafting some fine Neoclassical furniture. Many consider the furniture he made during the last years of his life his best. His son, Thomas the younger (1749-1822), kept alive the family tradition of superb furniture.

Photograph courtesy of Skinner, Inc.

The way the gentleman is discreetly portrayed on this plaque reveals Mr. Wedgwood's sense of propriety.

Even Mr. Wedgwood came up with china in a Neoclassical motif. He invented Jasperware with its white Classical figures on a blue background. There was only one non-Neoclassical touch added as a concession to modesty. There is a story that Mr. Wedgwood did not want to shock the ladies who bought his vases or candlesticks. He was concerned that if the figures were portrayed in genuine Classical "costumes," it might offend the ladies. So fig leaves were added in the appropriate places to some of his Jasperware.

Mr. Adam is a god in the world of antiques because he brought Neoclassicism to Britain and ultimately to America. In France, this look was called *le gout Grec* (Greek taste) and furniture was called the Louis XVI style in honor of Louis XVI of France.

Back in Britain Mr. Adam designed some pretty remarkable Neoclassical buildings, making him the Frank Lloyd Wright of

Photograph courtesy of Skinner, Inc.

This table is a perfect example of the Neoclassical styling of Louis XVI furniture. Notice the column shaped legs and the urn in the center of its stretcher.

Photograph courtesy of Skinner, Inc.

These mahogany shield back chairs from 1800 are the definitive example of Hepplewhite style with their urn shaped backs and square tapered legs.

the 1700s. His buildings, such as the partially destroyed Adelphi Terrace development in London, were famous for arches and vaults reminiscent of the glorious Roman temple, the Pantheon, famous for its vaulted roof. He also designed Neoclassical furnishings. Today Mr. Adam is mostly revered as a Neoclassical architect. Two of his apostles took his designs and wrote books about furniture. So here are two more wonderful antiques styles.

Do not panic! They are Neoclassical looking.

George Hepplewhite (?-1786) learned the art of furniture making in Lancaster, England, and like Mr. Chippendale and Mr. Wedgwood, went to London to make big pounds. Not much is known about him, and no furniture by him or his firm has been identified as coming from his hands.

In 1788, his widow, Alice, who continued the business, published his *The Cabinet Maker and Upholsterer's Guide.* The second edition came out in 1789 and the last in 1794. The preface of his book truthfully says that he is not an originator of designs but gives credit to Robert Adam for the Neoclassical style.

The most striking feature of the Hepplewhite style is its delicate look. His furniture was fragile looking when compared to Chippendale's English style or the earlier Queen Anne style. Hepplewhite furniture uses mahogany, and his furniture was mostly petite chairs or writing desks.

Hepplewhite style is truly Neoclassical. Besides the column, another famous artifact of Roman and Greek art is the urn.

Photograph courtesy of Skinner, Inc.

Even Mr. Hepplewhite had his version of the wing chair. His dates from 1790.

These ceramic pieces almost became the emblem for the Neoclassical look. They were crafted out of wood or brass and used as finials to decorate the top of bookcases and grandfather clocks. This motif in his chairs is probably what made Mr. Hepplewhite a legend. His design on seating equipment is his masterpiece and makes it easy to spot the Neoclassical look. The back of the chairs are shaped like Roman or Greek urns or shields. Hence, shield-back chairs.

The Hepplewhite style gave furniture legs a new look. It was not necessarily an improvement from others but rather another terrific leg design. Hepplewhite furniture had square-shaped legs that gradually got narrower or tapered to almost a point the closer it got to the leg's foot. At the foot, it would jut out slightly on all four sides to look like a square-shaped shovel. So Hepplewhite square-tapered legs with spade feet became a perennial favorite for many antiquers.

Mr. Chippendale liked carving but not Mr. Hepplewhite. Robust looking ball and claw feet and other carving would not look in proportion to the more fragile Hepplewhite pieces. He preferred the process of inlaying different colored pieces of wood in the mahogany as decoration. Marquetry is something like a mosaic of wood to embellish furniture. Mr. Hepplewhite liked an inlay depicting bell flowers, a popular motif whose name describes exactly what it is.

Regard this chair as one that had its wings clipped. Often called a lolling chair due to is comfort, this Hepplewhite prototype dates from 1800. Through the years they have acquired the lovely but inappropriate name of "Martha Washington chairs." There is strong evidence that Mrs. Washington never had such a chair.

Photograph courtesy of Skinner, Inc.

Mr. Hepplewhite's big invention was tambour fronts. These were small flat strips of wood pasted onto a heavy cloth that held them together. This made the wood flexible. Mr. Hepplewhite used these vertically on small writing desks something like an upright wooden curtain to hide the little cubby holes. The horizontal roll top seen on 1900s oak roll-top desks is the grandchild of Mr. Hepplewhite's vertical tambour.

A contemporary of Mr. Hepplewhite was Thomas Sheraton who was born in Stockton-on-Tees in 1751. Around 1790, like

Photograph courtesy of Skinner, Inc.

This American mahogany desk from the early 1800s is pure Hepplewhite. The square tapered legs with inlay/ marquetry on the leg fronts depicting bell flowers follows the designer's lines. The vertical panel of small upright wooden pieces is the tambour front invented by Mr. Hepplewhite.

Sideboards are to the Hepplewhite style what highboys are to Queen Anne. This is from 1800, and of course, is crafted from mahogany.

Photograph courtesy of Skinner, Inc.

the rest of his fellow antiques legends, Mr. Sheraton went to London. He was a skilled cabinet maker, but no furniture actually created by him has ever been identified. None of that matters because he published (you guessed it) his book in four parts from 1791-1794, *The Cabinet Maker and Upholsterer's Drawing Book.* He clearly stated that his book was a "cook book" of furniture designs exhibiting "the present taste of furniture." He also gave suggestions for the actual construction of pieces. His book was much used in Britain and helped bring the Neoclassical look to the newly independent United States.

Since both Hepplewhite and Sheraton styles are Neoclassical and use mahogany, they resemble each other. This makes it sometimes difficult to tell the difference between them. Sheraton begins with the letter "s" and has chair backs whose shape begins with the same letter as in square-shaped. The "white" part of Hepplewhite's name has the same two first letters as in

Photograph courtesy of Skinner, Inc.

An 1810 Sheraton version of a sideboard with the trademark rounded legs.

Photographs courtesy of Skinner, Inc.

The legs on these two tables illustrate the difference between the Hepplewhite and the Sheraton styles. The Pembroke table on the left follows the Hepplewhite style with square tapered legs. The cherry table on the right has rounded, lathe turned legs in the Sheraton style. Both are American and date from about 1800.

"wheel." Wheels are round, and Hepplewhite chairs have rounded or urn-shaped backs.

This trick for remembering the shape of chair backs is the opposite for legs. Hepplewhite advocated the square-shaped leg, and Sheraton used rounded legs. All this is confusing. It certainly was in the late 1700s and early 1800s for many cabinet makers. Even though they followed the two masters' books, things got mingled. Hepplewhite shield-shaped back chairs got mixed with rounded legs and so on.

Loomism: Do not worry if it is Hepplewhite or Sheraton. Think of it as "Heppleton." You will still be ahead of 99 percent of the adult population. Just remember this: Heppleton's trademarks were Neoclassical, square-tapered legs, or rounded legs with incised fluted carving, round or square backs.

Please take this affectionate nickname seriously because Yankee cabinet makers really became confused and mixed the elements of the two styles and created Heppleton pieces.

There is a habit in the United States of labeling American made Hepplewhite or Sheraton furniture as Federal. That is the

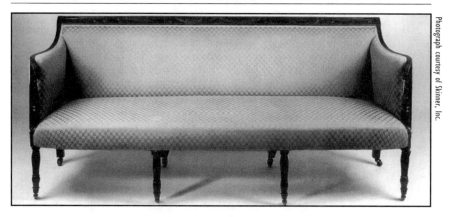

Photograph courtesy of Skinner, Inc.

Here is a sofa that quite possibly could have been made by Duncan Phyfe, the "Chippendale" of America. The exposed parts are mahogany with carved stalks of wheat on the center of its top horizontal panel, a popular Neoclassical motif. This sofa often gets labeled "Federal," or "Duncan Phyfe" styles. Both designations are confusing since no such furniture style actually exists. Better to say: "Sheraton style sofa from the Federal era or from the studio of Duncan Phyfe."

same mistake as labeling English pieces Georgian. Federal refers to the era when America's national government started in the 1790s. It is not a furniture style. We all agree that the term Federal does sound ritzy, but use the other terms, Hepplewhite, Sheraton, or "Heppleton."

In New York City in the early 1800s, a cabinet maker, Duncan Phyfe (1768-1854), carried out the Neoclassical designs of Sheraton and Hepplewhite to perfection. Duncan Phyfe is famous for his card tables with flip-flop tops that when opened doubled the surface area. Mr. Phyfe used lyres, another favorite of Neoclassical design, made out of mahogany as the base for some of his tables. Today American museums hoard his work, but you can find 1930s copies at most antiques malls or shops

Sheraton and Hepplewhite, or our "Heppleton" style continued to about the 1820s in the United States. Then the next style, still very Neoclassical, took over the country. It was so widespread that when one famous American was portrayed in sculpture, the knickers he usually wore were replaced by a Roman toga. Before that, let's learn about an English silversmith who beautifully duplicated Neoclassical designs.

13

Another 1700s Achiever

When learning about antiques, it seems there is a tendency to make certain generalizations. The first is that the trendsetters throughout time were the ladies, and usually royal ones. Those Queens, Anne, Victoria, and the less famous Charlotte (America's last female monarch before our Revolution) are on the list of fashion setters. George III's wife really pushed Wedgwood's career upwards when she ordered a set of his china for George and her family. Then there were the French Empresses, Josephine with her Empire style, and later her granddaughter-in-law Eugenie and her Rococo Revival tastes. Mary Todd Lincoln and fictional Scarlett O'Hara were two instigators of fashion who tried in the mid-1800s to "Rococoize" America.

Those are the famous female fashion rulers of history. In fairness, there were a few gentlemen. George IV, known as Regency George, brought Josephine's Empire style to England. He did it to anger his dad, George III, who was constantly battling Napoleon. The Regency era would be quite blah without the French influence that he made fashionable in England.

We Yanks have Thomas Jefferson who brought to America anything French. He served fine French wine and introduced the Parisian manner of having beds built into an alcove rather than standing in the center of a bedroom. So it is clear that both ladies and gentlemen were fashion dictators. That

Photograph courtesy of Cincinnati Art Museum.

This Neoclassical teapot from 1787/1788 by Hester Bateman is in the permanent collection of the Cincinnati Art Museum. It shows the fine craftsmanship and design that Mrs. Bateman put into her pieces.

ends the myth about females being the only gurus of chic.

Another generalization is that women did not participate in business affairs. It appears that the gents controlled the furniture and china fields. Hepplewhite, Sheraton, Spode, Chippendale, and Wedgwood all were of the male gender. Some potters did indeed checkout their patterns with their "significant other." One can almost hear Mrs. Wedgwood saying, "No, Josie, better stick to the blue and white. Women will like that better." In fact Mr. Wedgwood often gave Mrs. W. credit for her good business advice.

Here is another generalization breaker and a very important person to antique furniture, Mrs. George Hepplewhite. After Hepplewhite died, his widow published his book about styles with great success. Mrs. Hepplewhite is the reason George is so esteemed today. Without that book, he would probably be forgotten.

When experts discuss the top English silversmiths during the 1700s, this name if not at the top, is usually in the elite first five. Yes, indeed, as wonderfully unusual as it seems, this celebrated silversmith was a lady!

Hester Bateman (1708-1794), after her husband died, took over the family's silver business and made it even more triumphant. This was not too common or very easy back then. Her silver pieces, whether a spoon or a teapot, were very Neoclassical. Her quality creations beautifully complemented the fashionable items of the 1780s such as Wedgwood Jasperware and Sheraton and Hepplewhite sideboards. Her teapots were usually helmet shaped with an engraved design of a Roman looking urn. A tea set from her shop was perfectly suited to grace a Hepplewhite or Sheraton sideboard.

Critics like to point out that Mrs. Bateman could not read or write. That is to her credit because even without a formal education she made the business very successful. Jonathan, her son, joined her in 1769 and took over when she retired at age eighty two. Her grandson joined the firm in 1805 and became the third generation of the Bateman family to be a silversmith. Just like his grandma, he was a good business person and adapted his work to public demand. He gave up the Neoclassical look perfected by Mrs. Bateman and created lavish Victorian-era pieces in the then popular Rococo Revival manner.

Hester Bateman remains an outstanding silversmith of any century, any country, and a role model of a person who achieved much despite many drawbacks. It is also wonderful that her triumphs destroy a misconception that women in the old days could not have as successful business careers as men.

Our Neoclassical story continues in the next section as it dominated the United States.

14

The Empire Style

The next style, Empire, takes the Neoclassical look, so popular with Heppleton furniture, to its fullest development. It was immensely popular in the United States. It lasted from 1810, the last days of the Sheraton and Hepplewhite styles, to 1850 with the birth of the Rococo Revival style. Its designs showed up everywhere from buildings, houses, and furniture to high-waisted dresses. Even statues became Empire style. Those dating from that era often portrayed George Washington without his usual 1700s knickers. Sculptors fashionably depicted our first president as a Roman emperor complete with toga.

The origins of the Empire style came from France. The French Revolution, dating from 1789 to 1795, became a blood-bath in which the instigators turned against each other. King Louis XVI and his wife, Marie Antoinette, probably welcomed their executions which ended their nightmare. Many beautiful objects were destroyed during the Revolution not only at the King's palace, Versailles, but at various chateaux or castles throughout France.

In 1795 a modified republic was created, and as you guessed, a new style of furnishings was born. Named after the new Republic, the Directoire was really just a continuation of the Louis XVI style. Then, as now, it is all hype. Since the last style was named after the beheaded king, cabinet makers had to come up with a new tag for the same old stuff. That was in order to keep furniture sales strong. Directoire was not only politically correct, but it also had a glamorous ring to it.

Photograph courtesy of Skinner, Inc.

This figurine made in Germany in the late 1800s recreates in Meissen porcelain Napoleon and Josephine on the way to their coronation.

In the late 1790s a young general, Napoleon Bonaparte (1769-1821), rose to power. By 1799 he overthrew the Directoire and started a military dictatorship. In 1802 he restored monarchy and made himself the ruler. However, he was much too smart to call himself king. He remembered what had happened to his predecessor. So Napoleon created the French Empire, and he chose a higher title than mere king. Napoleon made himself emperor of the French.

Napoleon really was not technically French. His family was from Corsica, an island that belonged to France but in heritage was more Italian. If that was not enough to give him an inferiority complex, there was one more situation. He was lower end nobility! He never forgot his humble origins, and that probably influenced his motive for declaring himself emperor.

On December 2, 1804, his coronation was held at Notre Dame Cathedral in Paris. Who could have been better than Pope Pius VII to crown him? Just as the pontiff was ready to place the crown upon Napoleon's head, the emperor irreverently grabbed it from him and proclaimed to the world his power by crowning himself emperor and then his wife, Josephine, empress of France.

In Britain and the United States, the Neoclassical styles of Hepplewhite, Sheraton, Louis XVI, and Directoire dominated the decorating tastes before the French Empire style arrived. As

Photograph courtesy of Skinner, Inc.

Here is where the number one design trademark of the Empire style was born, the Sphinx himself along the Nile River in Egypt. Notice the claw feet clearly discernible in Eric Pape's painting.

you know, ancient Greece and Rome were the main sources of anything related to Neoclassicism. Although Egypt was part of the classical world, the public was more interested in the ruins of Pompeii that had been discovered in the mid 1700s. Egypt's wonders were overlooked until Napoleon's troops conquered it for France in 1798. Suddenly Egypt became the trendsetter in the early 1800s as Pompeii had been in the 1750s. The French Empire style was born.

The Empire style really was a continuation of the Neoclassicism of the Louis XVI style and the short-lived Directoire. However, there were some differences. Empire designs were heavier, gaudier, and most importantly, they included Egyptian touches. The main trademark of the Empire style was claw feet. The idea came from the Egyptian Sphinx which resembled a lion with the head of a Pharaoh. Those stone monuments dating from the time of the Pharaohs fascinated the French troops. It was those lions' feet that captured the public's fancy. Eventually their design was translated into furniture decoration. Claw feet were made out of wood or ormolu, a mixture of brass and other metals, to look like gold. They were used as feet for chairs, table legs, and other furnishings. Often they held a castor hidden in their hollow underside which made moving furniture easier.

Mahogany was the wood of the Empire style. Furniture was

heavier looking than in previous styles. Empire, which was the result of Napoleon's struggles for power, was literally a war-like style. Tables often looked like drums, and rooms were decorated with striped wallpaper reminiscent of military tents. This idea came from the temporary canvas quarters that housed soldiers during battles. Probably another reason for the military look was that Napoleon constantly wanted to remind everyone of his power. He did not want to get a close shave like poor Louis and Marie.

Empire furniture used much ormolu as ornamentation. Besides being crafted into claw feet, it was added as decoration to drawer fronts such as a wreath of leaves, another popular French Empire motif. Ormolu, a mixture of metals to resemble gold, was also known as bronze doré or golden bronze. It protected the wooden parts from being scratched. Pieces were frequently moved from country home to Parisian town house where its noble owner had to pay court to the emperor.

Perhaps the greatest trendsetter in the world of antiques was Napoleon's wife, the Empress Josephine. A gracious hostess, she was especially kind to the relatives of Louis XVI when they returned to France during her husband's reign. She also had great taste. Her mansion, Malmaison, near Paris, is Empire heaven. This happy house presents French Empire at its best. The decoration is very Greek, Roman, and especially Egyptian looking.

Photograph courtesy of Skinner, Inc.

This early Empire table circa 1820 is American but purely follows the French Empire. Called a pier or sometimes a "primping" table, the story goes that ladies checked their skirts in the looking glass. If it had been crafted in France, its columns and hairy animal claw feet would have been made in ormolu rather than carved from gilded wood.

A late 1800s portrait on German porcelain of the Empire trendsetter herself, the Empress Josephine of France.

Photograph courtesy of Skinner, Inc.

When walking into her dining room with its black and white marble floor, you can feel her presence and almost smell the champagne from her parties. Outside, her gardens glow with roses that are descendants of her original ones.

Napoleon himself would agree that the end of his career started when he divorced Josephine because their union had produced no child. He married Austrian Marie Louise (the niece of Marie Antoinette!) in order to have an heir. This alliance yielded a son who sadly died at an early age. Fate is tricky. Josephine's daughter, Hortense, from her first marriage, married Napoleon's brother, Joseph. Hortense and Joseph's son continued the fame of Napoleon. (Of course that is another antique style in a future chapter.) Napoleon had one defeat after another and finally died in exile in 1821. His and Josephine's Empire style lived on in France, Britain, and the United States.

Before leaving France, here is a story about the French "Chippendale," Georges Jacob (1739-1814) who was as adaptable to changing tastes as Mr. C. This cabinet maker made furniture starting in the mid 1700s during the reign of Louis XV. He flourished during the days of Louis XVI, the Directoire, and finally under Napoleon. Experts say that his last works in the Empire style from the early 1800s were his best.

During this time, Napoleon's main enemy was the British. Britain and France were in a series of wars from 1793 to 1815.

Photograph courtesy of Skinner, Inc.

This English sideboard, often called Regency after George IV of England, is basically Sheraton style except that it is bulkier than earlier ones. The brass rail in the rear of its top held a small curtain that was drawn when the sideboard was in use protecting the wall from splashes.

Besides war concerns, George III and Queen Charlotte fretted about their son, the Prince of Wales. Later known as George IV, he was quite a philanderer and did much to upset them. One way to antagonize his parents was to furnish his London home, Carlton House, with the latest from Paris. Soon the London swells followed his example. Empire dresses with high waistlines, along with Empire furniture, appeared in the best sitting rooms, not only in Britain, but eventually in the United States.

Since the Brits were constantly battling the French, this new style in England was not called Empire. That would have been bad policy. After all, you cannot name your furniture after your arch enemy. It was probably called the "Greek or Antique style." Today, English furniture dating from the early 1800s is often called "Regency." It followed the Neoclassical designs of French Empire, Hepplewhite, and Sheraton. However, this slightly different variation of the Classical theme was more massive looking than those three styles. The term Regency originated from the years 1811 to 1820 when the future George IV acted as king or regent for his insane father, George III. Think of Regency as English Empire furniture with touches of

Hepplewhite, Sheraton, or our "Heppleton." Visualize shield-back chairs with square-tapered legs.

In 1807 a famous novelist, Thomas Hope, published his book, *Household Furniture and Interior Decoration*, which summed up the furniture designs of his fabulous mansion. The furniture was basically French Empire with British interpretations. It favored straight lines, dark, glossy woods (especially mahogany) with ormolu ornamentation. Of course, there were those famous claw feet and columns.

Why aren't we calling furniture from that era by the person's name who created it? Here is another exception. It seems that the cabinet makers during the early 1800s did not catch the public's fancy as those big three of the 1700s. So English Empire-style pieces from the late days of George III or during the reign of George IV are still called Regency.

As Regency took place in England, what kind of furniture was popular in the early days of the American Republic? Hepplewhite and Sheraton were still popular even though of English origin.

Remember how historians call the early days of our country the Federal Period (1790-1825), when our national government was being established from the thirteen colonies. American-made Sheraton-style, or Hepplewhite-style furniture dating from those days is sometimes called Federal. As explained in the last chapter, use this expression for historical purposes and not as a term for furniture styles. Stick to calling pieces dating from that era as Sheraton, Hepplewhite, or our "Heppleton."

Photograph courtesy of Skinner, Inc.

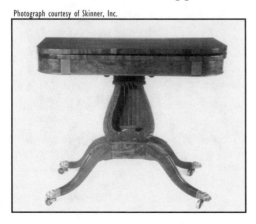

An American mahogany card table circa 1812 whose top flips open to double its surface, is a perfect example of the Neoclassical/Empire style. Its lyre base was inspired by Roman motifs. Its claw feet are made from brass.

In the 1790s following President Washington's advice, the United States tried to be neutral and avoid "entangling alliances." Americans at this time felt great hostility towards Great Britain and much admiration for things French. Yankees craved French wine, cuisine, art, and, of course, furniture. France was well-liked because its king, Louis XVI, helped fund the costs of our revolution. That happened not out of love for democracy but for hatred of his rival, King George III. Our third president, Thomas Jefferson, was a great Francophile, meaning he loved France. He had been minister there just before the French Revolution. His love of that country made anything France chic for Americans.

The bad feelings between Britain and the United States resulted in the War of 1812. On August 24, 1814, British troops arrived in Washington D.C. to burn the Executive Mansion and other public buildings. Everything in the president's home from armchairs to soup tureens were destroyed—except for one treasure. That wonderful first lady, Mrs. James Madison, just before escaping the burning house and British soldiers, rescued one of America's most beloved antiques. Moments before flames took over, she cut the portrait of George Washington by Gilbert Stuart from its frame and ran with it under her arm to her carriage. The Executive Mansion was later rebuilt. Its charred stone walls were painted white, and it eventually became known as the White House. How indebted we are to Dolly for saving that famous portrait of the father of our country!

Photograph courtesy of Skinner, Inc.

This German version of the Empire style, Biedermeier, from the early 1800s has, of course, those famous hairy claw feet and is made from light colored wood.

It is easy to understand how things British were not as well-received as anything French. When the latest furnishings from London arrived in America, merchants thought calling the furniture by its British name, Regency, would make it unsalable.

So some clever retailer came up with the idea of calling it by its French name, and the Empire style took the young nation by storm. After winning the War of 1812, Americans regarded their country as an empire marching westward from the East Coast across North America to the Pacific. Empire design trademarks soon were everywhere.

American Empire was fashionable from about 1810 to as late as 1850. When dealing with dates for furniture styles, always remember they are never exact. To be safe it is best to use our antiques word "circa," meaning approximately. Everything from bank buildings with Grecian-looking columns to card tables with harp- or lyre-shaped bases was done in this style.

American Empire is slightly different from French Empire. This seems perfectly logical. After all, America was more British than French in its heritage. American is less ornate and uses more carving rather than ormolu as decoration. By the 1820s the claw foot, instead of being crafted from ormolu as the French did, was usually carved from wood.

Popular motifs were pineapples carved in the midsection of table bases, and cornucopias or horns of plenty, often seen on the sides of scrolled-end sofas. Acanthus leaf carving was also popular. This design of leaves invented by the ancient Greeks was placed on legs of tables and chairs.

American Empire furniture used mostly mahogany and was dark and massive. Crotch mahogany veneer covered less expensive pine on drawer fronts. These beautifully grained thin strips of wood came from the parts of mahogany trees where a limb joined the trunk or twin trunks met at the fork or crotch. The grain usually had a feather-type design. Often the sides of chests of drawers were created from less expensive solid cherry that had the same color as mahogany. This was the era and style when cherry earned its nickname "poor man's mahogany."

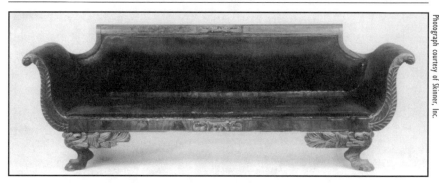

Photograph courtesy of Skinner, Inc.

This sofa is an example of early Empire style. Notice its detailed carving of cornucopia, acanthus leaf, and claw feet.

Let's define the Empire style in an American-made piece of furniture. To visualize American Empire we will look at three periods for an Empire sofa—early, middle, and late.

Early Empire

Early Empire was circa 1810 to circa 1830. A totally hand-made sofa is very ornate compared to later versions. It has finely carved, hairy animal claws as feet and cornucopia carving on either side of its front arms. This sofa, whether upholstered in velvet or horsehair, was considered very chic and quite upscale for those days.

Middle Empire

A Middle Empire version of this sofa dates circa 1830. This sofa looks like a photocopy of the earlier one and is a transitional piece. Earlier versions were totally handmade, and later ones

Photograph courtesy of Skinner, Inc.

This pier table is slightly younger than the one on page 118. It reflects the early machine manufacturing that was started during the day of the late Empire style. There are no claw feet or acanthus carving to be seen.

Photographs courtesy of Skinner, Inc.

On the left is an 1820 work or sewing table. It is clearly early Empire due to its detailed carved claw feet. On the right is the same type table in the late Empire manner from about 1840. Instead of carved feet, this machine made version has turned feet.

were almost always factory produced. However, this sofa was partially machine made, probably under a factory system of piece work. Possibly some of the insides of the frame, hidden under the upholstery, was also crafted by machine. The carving on the claw feet and arms has a flatter less-detailed look because it was done under "the faster is better" idea of mass production. The carver on the assembly line took less time than the cabinet maker had on the earlier sofa with its crisper detailing.

Late Empire: The Pillar and Scroll Era

Now comes the third period which marks a turning point in antiques. The Late Empire style of the 1840s is noteworthy because it is the first furniture style in the United States to almost be totally machine made. Being mass-assembled, our Late Empire sofa has less detailing than the earlier two versions. By comparison, the carving on Early Empire claw feet looks less clear, somewhat on the order of a photocopy of the original. The Late Empire sofa is a copy of a copy!

Here is how bulk-produced Late Empire pieces came to acquire an unflattering nickname. By the 1840s the Industrial

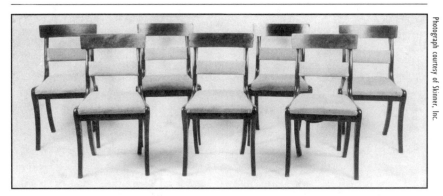

Photograph courtesy of Skinner, Inc.

A suite of late Empire side chairs of mahogany veneer over pine that dates from about 1830-1840. As totally machine made pieces they lack carving such as claw feet or acanthus leaves.

Revolution had blossomed in America. Glass objects such as water goblets and clocks, and silverplated items like teapots, as well as furniture, were mostly machine made. Wood-carving equipment of the 1840s was not yet perfected and could not accomplish the fine craftsmanship seen on earlier pieces. Machines could not yet do intricate work as required to produce the hairy animal claw feet on sofas. When trying to make this Empire trademark, the claw was shaved of all features, leaving only the outline of a scroll shape in the wood. Another example is the handcarved Neoclassical column. These posts decorated the fronts of chests of drawers of Early Empire pieces. When done by machines in the 1840s, they became s-shaped scrolls.

By the time a copy is made from a copy, the crispness and other details are gone. As a result, Late Empire pieces ended with the shape and outline of claw feet, or pineapple carving, or columns that the machine tried to duplicate. Since claw feet ended up as scroll ones, and columns wound up as pillars, Late Empire style was given the uncomplimentary nickname, Pillar and Scroll.

Late Empire in the 1840s, unlike earlier versions, became very affordable for the growing middle class, and it graced many parlors across America. This is the first furniture style identified with the Industrial Revolution and with the middle class. These two factors grew more powerful as the 1800s continued.

The rise of power of the middle class in the United States is very important in the study of antiques. Before the mid-1800s the blue stocking set ruled this country. One could hardly call Jefferson, Washington, or Monroe "one of the guys."

When Andrew Jackson was elected president in 1828, things changed. He was not from the Eastern shore but rather a "westerner" from the frontier of Tennessee. "Old Hickory" would be the first to proudly admit to his nonpatrician beginnings. His presidency has been called the "First Age of the Common Man," another way of saying the rise of the middle class. During his term, furniture, for the first time in America, was beginning to be mass-produced. This is an important part of the "First Age of the Common Man."

Late Empire furniture created in factories was displayed in stores, lined up for the shopper. It meant greater selection, no waiting for fabrication, and lower costs compared to handcrafted pieces. It also ended: "Oh, I know that should be in mahogany, but would you make mine in walnut with a little curlicue carving here?" The age of individuality was dying due to mass production.

Today this furniture has less clout with elite or Group I collectors than 1700s pieces, but who cares? Remember, Late Empire pieces qualify as genuine antiques by everyone's standards because they are about 150 years old. They are also well made and quite a deal when compared to the costs of their 1700s cousins. Malls and shops usually have several pieces of Late Empire furniture such as an 1840s card table. The price of $750 is more affordable than the thousands asked for a 1780s one. The furnishings produced during the "First Age of the Common Man" are genuine antiques ready to be treasured by "the Common Person," a very late twentieth-century way of saying Group II antiquers. That is the joy of Empire furniture.

We are about to meet an American who became a big success during the days of the Empire style.

15

An 1800s Achiever

Here is an American success story in the world of antiques. This is a really special one because it did not happen in England or in New York but in the heartland of America.

This achiever's story is about Mr. Henry Boyd (1802-1886), a famous American cabinet maker. He was born into slavery, and as a young boy worked for a cabinet maker. He bought his freedom at eighteen and moved to Cincinnati in 1826. At thirty-four, he became the proud owner of his own bed-making factory. By 1850 he had twenty employees.

Photograph courtesy of The Furniture Makers of Cincinnati 1790-1849, 1976

An advertisement for Boyd's beds from the June 27, 1843 Cincinnati Daily Gazette.

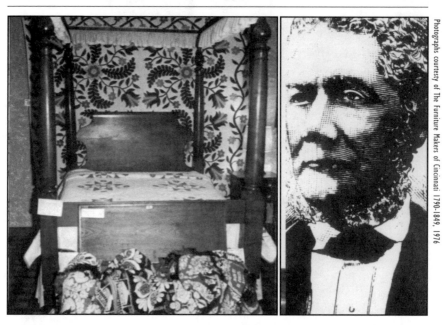

Photographs courtesy of The Furniture Makers of Cincinnati 1790-1849, 1976

Left: An example of Mr. Boyd's beds can be seen in the Golden Lamb Inn located in Lebanon, Ohio. Right: An engraving of Henry Boyd, an innovative furniture maker of the mid 1800s.

Mr. Boyd, a self-made man like Mr. Wedgwood, had that wonderful recipe for success. He combined business sense and artistic talents. He did not invent something totally new but perfected an existing piece of furniture. Jane Sikes Hageman wrote in her book, *The Furniture Makers of Cincinnati,* that in 1839 Mr. Boyd advertised that his line was "warranted to be the best beds that were ever made." He

Photograph courtesy of The Furniture Makers of Cincinnati 1790-1849, 1976

The master's name stamped on his bedpost: "Henry Boyd, Cin., Ohio."

A close-up showing the strong construction of a Boyd bed.

Photograph courtesty of The Furniture Makers of Cincinnati 1790-1849, 1976

really was not boasting but simply telling the truth. While other beds often collapsed, his versions never did, thanks to his improved construction.

Mr. Boyd made his beds from walnut, cherry, maple, and mahogany. He followed the Sheraton style with rounded testers and canopies. Those good looks were only the icing. His ingenuity was in the way beds were put together. The side horizontal piece and the baseboard or headboard on most beds were literally held together with a screw. Sometimes they got loose and resulted in not-so-gentle falls. Boyd's side piece hooked onto the headboard or baseboard, much the way modern beds do. The result was sturdy beds.

Many of Mr. B.'s competitors stopped making beds and advised clients to buy his. Boyd's products are an early example of mass production. In 1843 Mr. Boyd began stamping his name on his beds. He retired at age 61 and must have enjoyed retirement because he lived to 84. This gentlemen is a true 1800s achiever and a terrific example of how the Industrial Revolution affected everyone's lives. Mr. Boyd ended the problem of beds falling down, and today the "Boyd-better beds" are eagerly collected antiques. Also eagerly collected is furniture produced by a contemporary group, highlighted in the next chapter.

16

Shaker Furniture

T ime and fate can create quite unforeseen legacies. When Ann Lee, founder of the Society of Believers in Christ's Second Appearance, left England in 1774 for America, she was concerned about the religious state of her brethren. What type of furniture she or her followers would be using was probably not a major worry. Eventually they settled in Watervilet, near Albany, New York. Her group became known as the Shakers because they shook or danced during religious services. By the 1840s there were about 6,000

Photograph courtesy of *The Shaker Chair.*

Shaker Village, Mt. Lebanon, N. Y. looking North.

A view of the Shaker village in Mt. Lebanon, New York in the late 1800s.

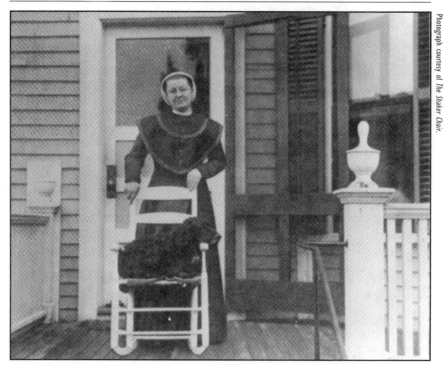

Photograph courtesy of *The Shaker Chair.*

A Shaker member, Mary Walker, around 1910, with her beloved pet and, of course, a Shaker rocking chair.

members with settlements in Maine, Vermont, Ohio, Rhode Island, and Kentucky.

Ann Lee would be amazed today to realize that the word "Shaker" more often designates upscale antiques rather than a holy society. Furniture created from her congregations helps keep alive the memory of her religious principles.

How tantalizing it is to learn how the Shakers got into the furniture business. Starting in the 1790s, practical furniture such as chairs or tables was crafted for the needs of the Shakers. A curio cabinet would never have been fashioned because it did not have a utilitarian purpose.

That cliché about "build a better mousetrap and the world will beat a pathway to your door" is true when it came to Shaker seating equipment. What had started as a "cottage industry" grew into a factory-type system that would even please Mr. Henry Ford. The settlement in Mt. Lebanon, New York

Photograph courtesy of *The Shaker Chair.*

The famous look of Shaker antiques:
a ladder back side chair hanging on
a wooden wall hook.

produced many chairs and marked them with a stencil saying
"Mt. Lebanon."

Chairs became the specialty of the Shakers and were eventually sold in neighboring towns and villages. Their most famous model is a slat back or ladder back. It was designed to hang like a hat, when not in use, from one of its slats on a wooden wall peg. They usually had a flame-shaped or acorn-type finial on each side of the chair's vertical back piece.

Another charming chair is called a "tilter." This version had in the base of its back posts an insert of ball and socket feet, so that the sitter could tilt backwards without hurting the chair's

Photographs courtesy of *The Shaker Chair.*

Here is the Shaker "tilter" chair. The detail shows the base of its back post with its ball and socket foot. This let the sitter tilt the chair back without damaging the chair.

Photograph courtesy of Skinner, Inc.

Many Shaker items such as boxes, scoops, and baskets are eagerly collected today.

frame. That soothing capability reveals that being highly strung is nothing new!

Experts say the peak years for Shaker furniture were from 1790 to the Civil War. Some were made as late as 1900. There was rarely carving or veneering on their creations. They certainly had those skills, but those "decorations" were deemed unnecessary.

Pieces usually followed the basic lines of Sheraton and Hepplewhite styles that were popular in the early 1800s. Local woods were used, cherry being the most popular. Their sewing or work tables, often called night stands, usually have those square-tapered legs designed by Mr. Hepplewhite.

Photograph courtesy of *The Shaker Chair.*

Charles R. Muller, author of *The Shaker Chair*, says: "The Shakers could make even the most mundane and utilitarian pieces dignified as well as sophisticated looking." This "convenience chair" from 1830 is a case in point.

This chest of drawers from the 1800s duplicates the light look of the Hepplewhite style furniture. Those square tapered legs would have pleased Mr. Hepplewhite. This piece is all the more amazing because it dates from the days when curlicue furnishing was most fashionable.

Photograph courtesy of Skinner, Inc.

Shaker pieces, whether a chest of drawers or a candlestick stand, all have that "naive furniture" flavor. Yet these furnishings are sophisticated and created by formally trained cabinet makers. Remember the lure of Shaker is its quality and understated elegance, not whether it was individually made.

Shaker furniture, even sometimes over 150 years old, seems as modern as if it were made yesterday. Others agreed. Mr. Gustav Stickley, making his furniture in the early 1900s, gave much credit to the Shakers for inspiring his designs.

Not only are Shaker antiques out of this world in demure loveliness, they come with another trait. As discussed earlier, antiques often possess sentimentality. Shaker ones have it jam packed. Webb Garrison in *Civil War Trivia and Fact Book* tells a tender detail

Photograph courtesy of Skinner, Inc.

This Connecticut piece which originally was built into a wall dates from around 1851. It cleverly combines a chest of drawers with an armoire, a novel idea that Art Deco furniture would do again about eighty years later.

This circa 1835 cherry and tiger striped maple chest of drawers looks very similar to a country Sheraton chest of drawers from the same era.

Photograph courtesy of Skinner, Inc.

about them. Shakers were pacifists but that did not stop them from helping victims of the conflict. After the War Between the States, a group in Pleasant Hill, Kentucky (a neutral state) reported they had fed over 50,000 soldiers—both northern and southern. Talk about getting an antique with terrific feelings. Imagine the warm vibrations from a Shaker piece that originated from there.

Shaker antiques are very chic and pricey. If buying Shaker, always have its authenticity in writing. Then sit back with confidence in one of those stress-reducing tilters and read in the next section about an important word in antiques.

17

Provenance:
All Show Business

Has this ever happened to you? As you debate whether to buy an antique, say, a chair, the seller sweetens its appeal by telling you its history. If you are in Chicago, perhaps you are told it came from the Marshall Field estate, as in famous department store people. In Baltimore a magnetic sales pitch would be that it once belonged to the Kirk family, the legendary silversmiths. Remember that line "George Washington slept here"? That exaggerated sales pitch probably helped sell many dilapidated properties.

These are all examples of the provenance of an antique. The history (provenance) of an antique is important. Collectors love antiques that once belonged to high profile folks such as famous

Photograph courtesy of Skinner, Inc.

Perhaps the charismatic of all provenances is when an object belonged to a movie star such as Garbo or Marilyn Monroe.

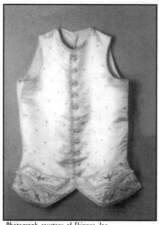

The family tradition that this late 1700s waistcoat was worn by Samuel Blagee (1762-1826), a Boston merchant makes it a four star antique for clothing collectors.

Photograph courtesy of Skinner, Inc.

movie stars or athletes. The fancy term for its ancestry, provenance, comes from the French meaning "source of origin." Think of provenance as the proven ancestry of an item. An antique's or a house's connection to a famous person makes it more desirable which, when translated into dollars, means more expensive.

Proving the history of ownership is easier if wills, appraisals, or household inventories exist. Dated purchase receipts also help to authenticate. Letters in which "great-grandmother Martha

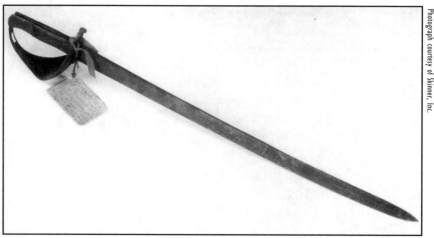

Photograph courtesy of Skinner, Inc.

A paper note attached to a mid 1800s cutlass and a bayonet saying it had been taken from a Confederate soldier in January 1865 makes this a highly desirable piece for Civil War buffs.

Photograph courtesy of Skinner, Inc.

The monogram "N" on these fine glasses does not stand for "Norton" but for the Emperor Napoleon III of France. That is a regal provenance!

Washington's chair" is mentioned can prove an item's pedigree. Never discount the handwritten note that some relative long ago placed upon a beloved heirloom.

The more famous the person, the more valuable the antique becomes. On November 15, 1990, Sotheby's in New York City auctioned artifacts belonging to the late Greta Garbo. One of her paintings by the French artist Albert Andre (1869-1954), "A Woman in White, Seated," sold for about $170,000. That was four times higher than any work by him had ever fetched at auction. It would seem logical that his pictures at later sales would be worth considerably more. It did not turn out that way. In November 1994, Sotheby's auctioned another of Andre's canvases that brought $23,000. Why did that other one go for so much? It is all "show biz." What a coup (and an expensive one) for its new owner to proudly say, "This painting came from the Garbo collection."

So you can see how the right type of provenance can really add bucks to the price of an antique. Who could possibly be more alluring than Garbo? You are right, Jackie Onassis! The auction of her possessions shattered logical price explanations. Even non-antique items reached astronomical amounts.

The *New York Times* reported results of the April 1996 sale at Sotheby's Auction in New York. A set of golf clubs owned by her first husband sold for $772,000, and a single putter went for

Photographs courtesy of Skinner, Inc.

For the academic antiquers here is the best provenance of all: a signed 1802 receipt from its maker to the first owner, Daniel Monore of Concord, Massachusetts. When brand new it cost $70. Skinner's estimated its auction price from $14,000 to $16,000. That receipt makes it more valuable.

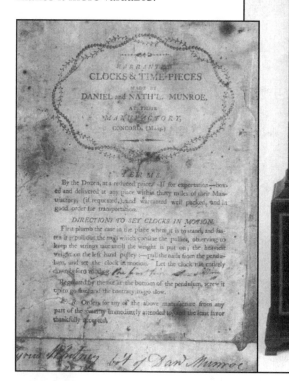

$65,570. That shows the eternal charisma of President Kennedy. A small box from the 1800s, a bonbonniere that holds breath sweeteners, was supposed to bring $2,000 to $3,000. However, since it belonged to Jackie, its winning bid was $14,950. That large amount could be somewhat justified. After all, it was gold and a genuine antique.

How do we rationalize the price of $211,500 for a set of fake pearls? Whew! They were supposed to bring $500 to $700. The Franklin Mint, the purchaser of the set, now sells the only exact reproduction of Jacqueline Kennedy's famous "faux," pearls. That certainly testifies to the appeal of the provenance of a famous person. It is also a hoot that savvy merchants translated "fake" into the ritzier-sounding French, "faux" to peddle those plastic beads.

Jackie's "pearls" are also a lesson on how not to let an item's provenance get the best of you, which can make buying at auction financially dangerous. Bidders often get too personally entangled with other buyers. They find themselves in that unsavory duo of the egos. Then they lose all control of their purse strings, resulting in paying far more than was necessary just because they wanted to beat the other person. That is how dimestore jewelry such as Mrs. O.'s ends up costing more than a fine French Impressionistic painting.

Buying antiques with a provenance is wonderful when one is a Group I Collector with unlimited funds. If your budget matches mine, try to avoid goodies that once belonged to the rich and famous. Or in more positive terms, be a Group II Collector and buy antiques without past associations. You will get more for less bucks. Then make yourself celebrated. Your antiques will suddenly have a pedigreed provenance and may sell for millions due to your fame.

All this talk of money brings to mind that we need more pointers about getting more antiques for our money; so, let's go on to the next chapter.

18

More Antiques Dash for Our Cash—Part II

Provenance is a word for Group II Collectors to avoid. Another term beginning with the same letter is pair, as we shall learn in our continued discussion on more antiques for our cash. It is no coincidence that those two words start with "p" as in pricey. Seriously, pairs of antiques are always more expensive than two comparable single ones.

Think Single

Whether a pair of 1825 prints, a pair of Roseville earthenware vases from the 1930s, or a pair of 1860s chairs, it doesn't matter. Because they are a pair, they cost more. Think in singles and make your own duos. For example, a pair of vases such as 1880s ones made by the Haviland firm in Limoges, France, retails for $250 because as a couple they are worth about 25 percent more. So a comparable single vase would retail for about $100. By purchasing two different but similar vases for $200, you have a savings of about 25 percent. And if one is chipped, the savings, as you know, can even be bigger. Just remember to place it high on the bookcase!

Avoid buying pairs or sets of anything antique in order to save money. This is especially wise pertaining to bedroom or dining room furniture. Matched sets called suites were made fashionable by the French since the mid-1800s. Purchasing piece by piece is not only economically smart but follows pre-1850s traditions. Homes of the 1700s were decorated

Photograph courtesy of Skinner, Inc.

Avoid the "P" words such as "Pair." These Chippendale style side chairs from about 1780 will bring a higher price as a "pair of side chairs" than they would if sold each by themselves.

with unmatched but similarly shaped and sized furnishings. There were no bedroom suites at Mount Vernon. In George and Martha's bedroom, the bed did not match the chest of drawers but all worked well together because they had similar proportions.

Neither did great-great-grandmother have a bedroom suite, but she had similar pieces in her room, although not exactly the same as in sets: a canopy bed, a chest of drawers, and a blanket chest. Purchase your antique dining room pieces except chairs in the same manner. Seating pieces are an exception to the generalization about sets. They have been made in bunches since the Middle Ages. Antique ones usually come in groups of four, six, eight, or even twelve; the more, the costlier. Instead of buying sets, find quality odd chairs that are about the same height and proportion. Buy an odd Hepplewhite side chair in the same reddish mahogany. Be sure that the Hepplewhite chairs have similar shield-shaped backs and those famous square tapered legs. When you get two or more, cover the seats in matching fabric.

You will be surprised how people will not even notice they are not a pair or a suite. That is the way people did in the old days. When one chair broke, they did not replace the whole set with brand-new chairs but only the broken one with a similar looking one. The savings can really add up. By acquiring six odd chairs instead of a matching set of six, you can possibly save as much as seventy-five percent.

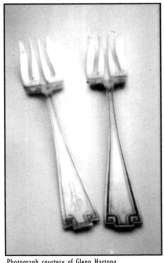

Silver flatware in Gorham's
"Etruscan" pattern.

Photograph courtesy of Glenn Hartong.

By finding each piece separately, you may have some antiques dollars left to buy some old silver flatware. When buying old silver choose monogrammed cutlery because it costs less than pieces without initials.

Yes to Monograms

Look at the two dinner forks at the top of the page. They were made by the Gorham Silver Company between 1913 and the early 1970s when this pattern, "Etruscan," was in production. It is very Neoclassical and at the same time very Art Deco looking due to its geometric design. The monogrammed fork on the left cost about $18 and the unmarked one was about $5 more. Who cares whose initials they are?

Be prepared for compliments on your silver. In these days of stainless steel and throw-away plastic everything, the use of silver flatware has become pretty special. When guests see those initials, they will ask if your cutlery is a family heirloom? Smile and say, "Why, yes they are family pieces." Then set the record straight. This is truly a form of reversed snobbism. Be proud of your deals. So truthfully add, "of course other peoples' families."

Anyway the savings are pretty amazing and still leave some dough left over to help furnish the dining area in your home.

Photograph courtesy of Skinner, Inc.

This lithograph by James McNeil Whistler (American 1834-1903) shows a high ceiling gallery at the Louvre Museum in Paris. Tall walls are a perfect place to hang pictures in need of repairs.

Novel Approach

Use our novel approach to antiques when looking for furniture. Perhaps you have a small dining room and are looking for a diminutive sideboard. Watch out, those little gems no matter from what era or what style are mighty costly. Why? Not many little ones were crafted in the old days of huge dining rooms, and today many want them for our continuously getting smaller dining areas.

Be inventive by using an alternative piece. A Sheraton style dressing table may work. This 1830s piece with its rope looking rounded legs and three little drawers on top a few years ago cost me $375. An 1830s similarly designed diminutive sideboard would almost be impossible to find, and if you did, expect to pay $3,000 or more. This dressing table holds flatware (monogrammed of course) just as stylishly as a more conventional sideboard. An Oriental rug would look mighty terrific underneath this dressing table or really with any antique.

Tears are Fine

Carpets from the Near East or the Orient have been made for centuries and go with anything from cabriole legs on a

Queen Anne lowboy to being used in front of the computer. The top-dollar ones are supposed to be made of thick wool, have no fading or tearing, have very tight, fine knots, and, of course, be untouched by pets. If one of these handwoven beauties is slightly torn or faded, the carpet can cost fifty percent less. Anyway, a really distressed one adds a little "family heirloom" look to our homes. Guests will always assume it was your great-grandmother's. As rugs acquire their small tears and fading, they seem to become more "weathered" looking, only adding to their appeal as antiques.

Problems Welcomed

Our "less than perfect" rule works well with other antique furniture. When a chest of drawers has replaced handles which in "antiquese" are called "pulls", it is usually priced twenty-five percent less than one with original hardware. Who can tell the original brackets from new anyway? Just make sure the replacements are good quality and similar in design to the piece. You do not want ornate Victorian-era looking ones on a more sedate looking country 1780s chest of drawers.

Heavenly Marriages

Well-made pieces of antique furniture such as cupboards and highboys are usually crafted in two pieces, top and bottom, not permanently joined in the middle. Corner cupboards usually have two-piece construction. Thank goodness, especially when it comes to moving, two pieces really make it a lot easier.

Purists want to make sure the top of a piece is original to the bottom. In other words, they were made for each other by the same cabinet maker from the same woods, design, and era. If not totally original, the first group of antiquers would pass by this beauty. Here is a really good example of getting more for our antiques dollars.

A friend bought a country cherry Queen Anne highboy made in Connecticut circa 1740 to 1780. It has cabriole legs, pad feet, and a scalloped design on its apron that stretches between its front legs. It cost $3,400. A fine reproduction could not be purchased for that figure. It seems that such a Queen Anne charmer should cost at least double or maybe triple.

This is a story about antique marriages. Its top is not original to the bottom, and the brasses have been replaced. It is what collectors call a "married piece." Group I people would tend to shy away from such matches. Both pieces were crafted about the same time and in nearby areas following the Queen Anne style, but undoubtedly by different cabinet makers. The two pieces were joined or married later. Highboys take a lot of room and perhaps at one time the top was taken off the original base and made into a tall chest of drawers by adding feet. The original bottom of the highboy minus top had a board in similar cherry put across its top surface. Presto, a rather over-scaled (too tall and too massive) but nonetheless pretty lowboy. Then later a top section missing its base was placed upon this base that had lost its upper section. A "married" highboy resulted.

For us bargain antiquers, this combination of top and bottom was a marriage made in antiques heaven. How are we sure it is a married piece? The best advice about successful antiquing is to always buy reputable retail, and you can safely collect.

You will hear me say this over and over, but it is the honest truth. When my antiquer pal fell in love at an antiques show with a married highboy, the dealer immediately explained its defects or problems. Then he smiled and said, "That is why I am only asking $3,400 for it." Here is a good rule about negotiating price. When a dealer gives you his best price on an item, and it's a good one, buy it for that. Do not try to get a lower one. That antiquer could never afford a Queen Anne highboy in almost perfect condition, so its imperfections made it possible for him to have it. That happy fellow calls it "the antique of my dreams." So married pieces can be a union made in Heaven because they allow Group II members an opportunity to acquire an antique if in almost pristine condition would be beyond most of our means.

Shop Safely

The final cautionary advice is to know an antiques defects before falling in love with it. Let's say you are at an auction and you see a highboy and you want to check it out. Ask the auctioneer questions at the preauction viewing. Look at the back of the two pieces. If married, the woods from the top and bottom do not match in color, alignment, and size. Also check out the dovetailing on the drawers on the top section and on the bottom. If the dovetailing is very different, watch out and be careful. If in doubt it is better to pass. Do not get too disappointed. You will find another gem to whet your antiques appetite.

Price Negotiation

In case you want to buy an item from a dealer, here are some things you need to know about antiques dealers. A lot of people seem to begrudge them a profit. An honest one is entitled to a fair mark-up. After all, the buyer is paying for the merchant's expertise, and remember that person has expenses such as rent and insurance. Sometimes an item may take a year or more to sell. Do not envy them a profit.

Here is another point. A few collectors like to say that most dealers are not totally on the up and up. Well, not true. Just get the dealer to put the description, age, wood etc. about the purchase in writing on the receipt, and you will be safe.

If the seller will not do that, then do not buy the item. Remember, there are other antiques in the sea of shopping.

When the dealers wrote the receipt for that married highboy, they put down all its problems: "Connecticut cherry highboy with fan carving, cabriole legs, circa 1760. Note: this is a marriage, both top and bottom are eighteenth-century pieces joined later, drops and brasses replaced." That is a splendid receipt because it told everything. Again, always buy from a reputable retailer. You may not get it for a song, but what you hope you're getting is actually what you are getting.

Layaway

And here is another reason dealers are so wonderful. Most offer the greatest invention for antiquers since the cabriole leg: layaway. A little dough up-front and then a few installment payments, and it's yours. That is a good way to buy high-end antiques.

Bargaining

Now on to the once-considered delicate subject of price negotiation. First of all, mellow out, it is no big deal. Maybe ten years ago it was, but certainly not anymore. These days everyone from the dealer to the buyer expects to bargain.

Getting a better price on antiques is less emotional these days because most of us shop at antiques malls. Most cashiers automatically deduct ten percent on items costing more than $10 or sometimes more than $25. If you want an even better price, ask the mall manager to call the dealer. Since most sellers are not in their mall space and we talk only to the manager, it makes the price game less emotional. The manager acts as a referee, a role similar to a real estate agent.

So hooray for dealers! They bring and display tantalizing goodies whether china, books, or furniture to us. So here are some tips on bargaining when you are talking directly to them. Remember this is a game to be played with gentility, and it is definitely not a war.

Pretend you're interested in a teacup and saucer. Look it over and ask important questions. Find out if it's English, porcelain, or earthenware, its age, and anything that may interest you. Then say "I really like it," and take a long p–a–u–s–e. This gives the dealer a chance to say "I can do better." That happens often. If you like the lower price, then take it. If not, offer less, about ten percent to twenty percent. Anything more will probably be taken as an insult. If you still do not like the price, it is better to quit. There will be other teacups and saucers.

Here is another suggestion for price negotiation which sounds better than saying haggling. This one involves using a friend, another example as discussed earlier of how antiques can build friendships. This tip evolved with the help of Pete and is called the "two for." Often he, his wife, or I like two different antiques in the same booth. At one show he wanted a drawing of a horse, and I loved a painting depicting red flowers in a blue and white vase. We asked the seller what kind of price he would do if we bought the two items. It was amazing what a good deal we got, about forty percent off, and what extra fun it is to buy things that way. "Two fors" aren't always possible, but when you can, give it a try. It seems everybody ends up happy. The two buyers get really good prices, and the dealer sells two things at the same time.

Here are some "avoiders." They only hurt feelings and end up making everybody angry when we are trying to have fun as we antique. If an item is priced $10 or less, pay the price. Don't negotiate. It is always tempting to try. It really is tacky and this antiquer has to constantly remind himself about this point. And never, never say "I will give you." Dealers justly hate this line. You are not giving anything, you are paying.

Also, don't knock the merchandise. Forget this technique: "You know I would like to buy this cut glass bowl but it is so badly chipped." That line was once used on me when I did estate sales. My reply with a smile, "You're right. I couldn't possibly sell it to you with a clear conscience."

Questioning the seller's knowledge is one sure way not to get a better price. What if the price ticket reads "Haviland china made in 1880," and you turn over one of the plates and on the bottom is clearly stamped "Made in France." You instantly know that means twentieth-century production. Do not argue age if you want a friendlier price. That ploy only turns off the seller.

Remember this whole question about prices is much easier than it seems. The best advice came from my antiquer Aunt Panny. She said, "You catch more flies with honey than vinegar."

In our case, you get more antiques at good prices with gentility, when negotiating, than by making the bargaining process a war.

One of the very best "honey" approaches is my all-time favorite line, "Is there any room for negotiation on your price?" It is a terrific approach that usually works. However, once a dealer responded this way, "What a lovely way to ask, but the answer is no." Her charming response brings up an important point. If a dealer gives you their best price, accept it or reject it tactfully. Don't try to further bargain. It is like the antique saying about beating a dead horse. Besides if a price is way out of line in your opinion, forget it. You will find something else equally appealing at a more realistic price.

One of the main misconceptions is that an antique item, such as a wooden mixing bowl, is the only one in the whole world for sale. Thanks to our patron saint of antiquing, Saint Josiah Wedgwood, there are plenty of antique mixing bowls for sale. It is true the choice is less plentiful than finding brand-new ones, but antiquing is more fun. So have patience, you will find your antique at a good price, probably sooner than you expected. The only suggestion is to put it on the back burner of your shopping list, and that way you will stumble upon it sooner.

By now we all should be on that promised "antiquer's high," ready for successful antiquing and equally eager to learn more about antiques. Remember they have been kissed by time. Consider those chips and dents as double bonuses: the weathered look makes them look like antiques, and at the same time makes them more affordable than ones in pristine condition. That brings up another point about liking antiques in less-than-perfect condition.

Have you ever been in someone's home whose antiques are so perfect they put the best museums to shame? Did you feel cozy there, or were you afraid to touch anything or even sit down? The defense for buying antiques in less than perfect condition rests its case. The next chapters tell us about an era when budgeting money was not as necessary as it is these days.

19

Rococo Revival

Mary Todd Lincoln and Scarlett O'Hara trying to out-decorate Queen Victoria and the Empress Eugenie is the best way to describe Rococo Revival.

The Victorian era is a time many regard fondly as "the good old days." The Big Three styles were: Rococo Revival, Eastlake, and the Renaissance Revival. These styles were in vogue simultaneously from about 1850 to 1890. Notice that two use revival in their names rather than saying Neo-Rococo or Neo-Renaissance. Neo and revival have the same meaning. The prefix neo is the more understated 1700s way, as in the Neoclassical style. To the Victorian ear, "revival" sounded better because it had a more elaborate ring. So most of the popular designs of the 1800s had revival in their titles. Even in the names of furniture styles, Victorians generally preferred the grander over the unpretentious.

Twenty or more years ago, followers of the pre-1820s rule for genuine antiques dismissed relics from this era as junk. Now all that has changed. Mementos from the 1800s are considered fine antiques with big price tags. Just chuckle and remember what one person considers trash, another loves as antique. Gram would always say to me, "Why do you want that? I threw one out just like it before you were born?" The antique is truly in the eye of the antiquer.

The death of George IV in 1830 marked the conclusion of the Georgian era, named after the four George Hanovers who

Queen Victoria, who ruled England from 1837-1901, is painted upon Limoges porcelain.

Photograph courtesy of Skinner, Inc.

ruled Britain from 1714 to 1830. His brother, William IV, reigned from 1830 until 1837. When he died without heirs, his niece Victoria became queen. The years of her sovereignty, 1837-1901, are called the Victorian Age. Just as there is no such thing as Georgian style, there is also no Victorian. Her rule witnessed many designs, but none officially used her name.

Victoria remains the most famous queen in modern history. Among antiquers she is right up there with Queen Anne. Americans tend to look fondly upon her epoch. Indeed it was a prosperous and progressive time for Britain, France, and America. The Industrial Revolution, besides creating great fortunes, also increased the size of the middle class. Of course, all was not wonderful. The United States endured the bloody tragedy of the War Between the States, and France had a horrendous struggle with Germany—the Franco Prussian War in 1870.

The 1800s witnessed numerous inventions such as tele-graphs, telephones, trains, and steamboats. Photography best

Photograph courtesy of Skinner, Inc.

This daguerreotype of a locomotive from the mid 1800s shows two inventions of the Victorian era that brought about the modern world: daguerreotypes and trains.

illustrates the advances made during the Victorian era. Before 1838 only a costly portrait captured the likeness of a person. Then the daguerreotype process conceived by Louis Daguerre and later breakthroughs made photos affordable for most. The same happened with other everyday items.

By the 1870s there were many American millionaires: Carnegie, Rockefeller, Vanderbilt, and others. Also the middle class and its buying power had multiplied. In the 1700s only a few could afford a chair by Mr. Chippendale or a silver teapot by Mrs. Bateman. By the 1850s the middle class was larger and more prosperous than ever. It was perfect timing because the explosion of home goods made by machinery, including everything from soap to washstands, matched the homemakers' strong buying power.

During the reigns of Victoria and the Lincolns on our side of the ocean, goods were so plentiful that the way merchandise was sold changed dramatically. Before the 1850s a customer went to many little shops—one for gloves, another for china, and so on. The Industrial Revolution transformed that. There were still small places, but emporiums selling various items under one roof popped up all over France, Britain, and the United States. Many consider the Parisian Bon Marché founded in 1865

Photograph courtesy of Skinner, Inc.

This 1868 painting by Frederick Dickinson Williams (American 1829-1915) captures how by 1868 Boston and much of the U.S. had become very industrialized.

the first true department store. A Chicagoan would argue Marshall Field did it first, and Philadelphians would proclaim John Wanamaker as the pioneer in retailing. These stores were established about the same time as the result of the Industrial Revolution. There were lots of newly prosperous people furnishing their homes with the latest goods.

Here is a look at the first big style of the Victorian era.

Loomism: Never call antiques made during Victoria's reign "Victorian style." We shall encounter several during our look at her reign.

Labeling an antique as Victorian is like saying all American guns made during President Lincoln's term were "Lincoln types." A more precise designation is a Spencer rifle or a Sharps rifle. Remember there is no Georgian-style furniture, rather Georgian-era furniture designed by Chippendale, Hepplewhite, and Sheraton. The same applies for several mid-1800s designs.

Rococo Revival is usually labeled Victorian. It was the rage in Paris from 1852 to 1870 when Napoleon III and the Empress

Photograph courtesy of Skinner, Inc.

This walnut parlor table captures Rococo Revival style with its cabriole legs and ornate curves.

Eugenie ruled France. How unexpected life can be. Napoleon III was the grandson of Empress Josephine from her first marriage. Remember how Napoleon I divorced the beautiful Josephine because she produced no male heir from their marriage? Then Napoleon had a son from his second union, Napoleon II, but he died early from tuberculosis. The mother of Napoleon III was Hortense, Josephine's daughter, and his father was Joseph, Napoleon I's brother. Royal genealogy does get confusing just like today's royal marriages and divorces.

To keep this story less confusing, think of Napoleon III of France as the grandson of Josephine. She would like that. We antiquers appreciate her for her tasteful influence upon the Empire style. Her grandson's rule is called the Second Empire. The term "Napoleon III" for French antiques is similar to the American and British designation "Victorian."

A look into French history during the early 1800s will help us understand the mentality of Rococo Revival. After Napoleon I was exiled, the French restored the monarchy. The two brothers of the beheaded Louis XVI, Louis XVIII, and Charles X ruled. Louis XVII, the young son of the king and Queen Marie Antoinette, died in prison during the revolution. Furniture crafted during the reigns of the executed ruler's brothers was called Restoration/Louis XVIII/Charles X in their honor. It basically followed the Napoleonic/Empire style. However, lighter colored woods such as cherry or pear were used instead of the mahogany favored in Empire. During the glory of Napoleon III and Eugenie, Paris was more than ever the center of the aesthetic world. People flocked there to study art, food, architecture, fashions, and furnishings.

In the 1840s the French looked into their history for design concepts. The Louis XVI style, was sumptuous but still recalled memories of bread lines and beheadings. The Louis XV/Rococo style was rediscovered. By then the cruelness of Louis XV was forgotten. Only memories of balls at Versailles and France being a world power lingered.

So the Louis XV/Rococo style from the mid-1700s was the perfect tonic for the Emperor and Empress and the growing and prosperous middle class. The goal was to proclaim wealth to the world through lifestyles, clothing, and especially home furnishings.

Rococo/Louis XV suddenly became the look for debonair Parisians. Continuing our antiques story "A Tale of Two Cities," Londoners as always soon followed. Then Mrs. Lincoln added a whole new twist when she tried to "rococoize" the Neoclassical White House.

That wonderful French expression, "the more it changes, the more it stays the same" is certainly true with Rococo Revival. You already know the style. Remember Mr. Chippendale published its designs in the mid-1700s. Then in the 1800s this style really took hold in Britain and America. Those well-to-do of late, just like their French counterparts, were so embarrassed at being self-made that they chose to show to everyone their financial triumphs through the ornateness of their homes and furnishings.

The three biggest trend-setters of the mid-1800s, Victoria, Eugenie, and Napoleon III, really endorsed Rococo Revival. Besides that, those rulers started the enduring friendship of France and Great Britain. Once enemies, today they remain buddies. As a token of goodwill, Victoria gave to France the wagon that held the coffin of the first Napoleon. That was a generous gesture because Napoleon I had wanted to conquer Britain. Today the cart is displayed at Malmaison.

Besides fashionability, Rococo Revival also had the bonus of being politically correct. The new camaraderie made it more desirable than ever for London to follow Paris. Then New York, Philadelphia, Chicago, and even Washington D.C. followed the same Parisian trends.

The Victorian age marks an important point in history. We can now look with affection at Great Britain without worry of disloyalty to our country. After the Civil War, the United States and Britain became and remain great partners in world affairs. That is pleasing. Was it rather awkward for you (as for me) trying to be hostile to the nation that is the home of Wedgwood, Spode, Chippendale, Queen Anne, and wonderful Victoria?

Besides world politics, there were other reasons Rococo Revival so successfully walloped the United States. With the

Photograph courtesy of Skinner, Inc.

How Victorians loved these *etagere* or what-not shelves. Today they are called curio cabinets. This walnut version was probably filled with small bric a brac from miniature glass shoes to ceramic statues.

tremendous rise of the middle class on both sides of the Atlantic, there came a new decorating philosophy. Pre-1840 styles were too understated for most Victorians. Take that "What kind of antiquer are you?" quiz again to understand the Victorian mentality.

To understand the Victorian era, visit the White House. It was "rococoized" in the 1860s by a southern lady who was a loyal Unionist, Mary Todd Lincoln. This residence dating from the early 1790s is Neoclassical. Its facade with columns and evenly spaced windows is the trademark of that style.

The interior of the house before Mrs. Lincoln was furnished basically with "Heppleton" and Early Empire furniture. The First Lady, feeling inferior because she was the wife of a lawyer from Illinois, wanted to be an equal to Queen Victoria and the Empress Eugenie when it came to glamorizing her home.

Clutter became the number one priority. "Fill and cram up as much as possible" became the decorating belief. Mrs. Lincoln followed Victoria's rule of twenty pictures per table. (Why settle for just one photograph on a table when nineteen more can be crammed onto it?) The East Room, once very Neoclassical with paneling, became "rococoized" with palm tress and competing floral designs. Motif on carpets, upholstery, and draperies fought each other. Mantels practically became curio cabinets loaded with *objets d'art*, then a fashionable French expression for pretty little things.

In the 1860s, Rococo Revival was called the "French Style." The name certainly fit the times. It was the "Gilded Age," as Mark Twain said in his writing. Nearly everything from ceilings to furniture had gold decoration, and the term was also used figuratively for the times. Using fancy-sounding French terms was a way of gilding one's speech as gold did to furnishings.

Anything French was considered "the last word." However, we antiquers are still paying the price for this "French" invasion. Describing antiques in that cultured tongue makes it more difficult to learn about them. Earlier we wisely decided to discard most French terms except that terrific one, "cabriole," as in Queen Anne legs.

However, there is one more French expression that should be retained. Simple and appropriate, "suite" means a matched set. It could be used for dining, parlor, or bedroom pieces. Around 1850 suites became widespread in Britain and the United States. Of course, matched chairs had been made for centuries. Victorians wanted everything similar from sanitary ware including china sets of chamber pots, pitchers, and bowls to bedroom suites with identically designed bed, washstand, and chest of drawers. Also, dining rooms could have myriad pieces including numerous chairs, server, sideboard, china closet, and table. Parlor suites consisted of a smallish sofa, one armchair for a gentlemen, a slightly smaller version for a lady, and perhaps two or three side chairs.

Do you recall how furniture before the Queen Anne style was cramped? So was this style. When Gram branded antiques as uncomfortable, she was probably referring to Rococo Revival pieces remembered from her childhood. She was right. The seats were little, the legs short, and although the backs were upholstered, they were stiff. The Victorians sat upon such "sitter beware" pieces on select occasions in the parlor with special visitors.

A Rococo Revival-style suite illustrates the two "R's" that define this style: rosewood and roses. Rosewood was now more

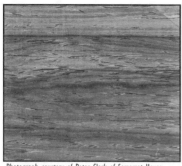

Here is the most fashionable wood of the Rococo Revival days, rosewood. Its background color is similar to mahogany but it has that very flamboyant black grain running through it.

Photograph courtesy of Peter Clark of Somerset House.

popular than mahogany which dominated 1700s furnishings. Walnut was the next favorite. Grown in tropical countries, rosewood had a background color resembling mahogany, but it had a flamboyant and striking black graining running through it.

The second "R" of Rococo Revival is for "roses." The top horizontal part of chairs or sofas often had carved roses in its crest. The cabriole leg was taken directly from the French Rococo/Louis XV of the 1750s and the Queen Ann style. Most were machine made and not as crisp or three-dimensional as handcrafted versions.

Chairs were usually grouped around a marble-topped table in the center of the parlor. White marble was considered the choicest because its paleness was a good contrast to the dark rosewood or walnut. Rococo Revival furniture had other carving besides roses, such as leaves, grapes, scrolls, or shells. Side chairs with rounded backs were called balloon backs.

Photograph courtesy of Skinner, Inc.

Two mid 1860s chairs of laminated rosewood by John Henry Belter of New York City. Mary Todd Lincoln and other Victorian ladies such as the fictional Miss Scarlet loved this style.

The names concocted for Rococo Revival pieces show the Victorian fervor for things French. Calling a curio cabinet by such a down-to-earth term would not do. They were baptized *etagere*–the French term for shelves.

The ultimate piece of Victorian frou-frou is an s-shaped settee, a *tête à tête*, meaning "head to head" in French. It resembled two chairs side by side joined at the armrest, facing opposite directions. This was even cozier than a conventional love seat because it allowed its occupants eye-to-eye contact. Using this French term seemed prudent. A little discretion was needed to camouflage its provocative function. Perhaps the Victorian era is not as prudish as once thought!

Before Rococo Revival's comeback among collectors, there was little information in antiques books about John Henry Belter (1804-1863) of New York City. This famous cabinet maker was to 1850s furniture what Chippendale was to 1700s designs.

Mr. Belter, a German immigrant, became the outstanding cabinet maker in the 1840s. His work reflects the technological advances of the Industrial Revolution. He perfected the lamination process. Several layers of thin strips of rosewood or walnut with the grain of each running in one direction in one layer and the opposite in the next were glued together. This resembled plywood, giving pieces strength, pliability, and lightness needed for the curvy shapes of his furniture. Panels were steamed in molds which then were shaped into those curly forms of Rococo Revival. Others duplicated his look, but Mr. Belter remains the master.

The first important style of the Victorian Age was Rococo Revival. It started about 1850 and lasted as late as the 1880s. It has become associated with hoop skirts, Scarlett O'Hara, Mary Todd Lincoln, the Empress Eugenie, and of course the lady herself, Queen Victoria. If you are ready to think this era was totally curlicue, you are in for an antiques surprise.

The Other Styles of the Victorian Era

If you are hooked on Rococo Revival, you probably have a Victorian spirit. Or if you are a little wary of its ornateness, you may still have a Victorian soul. Not everyone in the late 1800s was enthralled with flamboyant decorating. During Rococo Revival's time, a design revolt began.

The most famous of the curlicue fighters was an English architect, Mr. Charles Lock Eastlake (1836-1906). He published in Britain in 1868 and in the United States in 1872, *Hints on Household Tastes.* This chap wanted to do away with ornate furnishings and preferred simple, sturdy pieces. As his earlier colleagues, Chippendale, Hepplewhite, and Sheraton, Eastlake had a style named after him following the ideas in his best-seller. As the Queen Anne style in the early 1700s brushed away excessive fussiness, so did Eastlake. Rococo Revival, although lacking spooky carving, was excessively sprinkled with carved roses, grapes, and cherubs. This was all unnecessary according to Mr. Eastlake.

Chests of drawers, sideboards, and other big pieces, now called Eastlake, usually had rectangular or boxy shapes and no curviness. Straight lines define its main trademark. Walnut and oak became as favored as they were before the age of mahogany. Mr. Eastlake felt that elaborate carving detracted from the beauty of the wood's grain, which should be the main decoration.

One of his ploys was to use veneered panels of burl walnut on the fronts of drawers. From the knots of walnut trees, burl

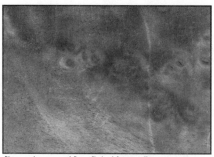

Burl walnut decorated many pieces of Eastlake style furnishing.

Photograph courtesy of Peter Clark of Somerset House.

walnut has a very visible grain with a concentric design. The decoration was a concession to embellishment on Eastlake pieces. The aim was to sell furniture, which meant pleasing the "too much is still not enough" decorating tastes of those Victorian folks. Chairs, marble-topped tables, or sideboards often had incised or low relief carving. This concave mark is cut into the wood by a machine. After scooping ice cream from its container, the hole left is an example of incised carving so similar to Eastlake details.

Its uncurvy lines and incised carving helped Eastlake adapt easily to mass production. So it became the "fast food" of furnishings. Its moderate cost made it affordable for most American homes whether farmhouses, suburban bungalows, or city apartments.

Eastlake parlor suites were very popular. They usually had one settee, two arm chairs, and at least two side chairs. Homemakers typically grouped them in the parlor around a marble-topped table following the same lines. Today collectors trying to recapture this 1870s flavor love to find those suites and reupholster them in Victorian colors such as deep rose or dark green.

Eastlake-style chest of drawers usually came in two sizes. The long low ones had two drawers, marble tops, and an attached mirror. The taller ones had three drawers and a central mirror atop a small area of marble. This was flanked on each side with handkerchief-sized drawers. The wooden side supports that held the mirror resemble the wishbone of a turkey, and now they are known as wishbone dressers. Eastlake furniture used deep red marble rather than the white seen on Rococo

Revival. That color complimented the brownish shades of walnut and oak.

This style became so well-liked that many American homes built in the 1870s and even as late as 1910 have Eastlake woodwork. The molding around doors or windows have designs similar to the incised carving of an Eastlake sideboard. An antiquer buddy calls this woodwork around doors "eggs and bacon molding." The corners have a circular design resembling fried eggs, and the long parts have incised carving resembling cooked bacon. Sometimes houses from this era have mantels matching Eastlake pieces.

The official years of Eastlake are about 1870 to 1890. It gets confusing because Victorians furnished their homes not exclusively with one style but often mixed them. An 1820s Empire

Photograph courtesy of Skinner, Inc.

This seven-piece bedroom suite from around 1870, although painted with a bird and floral design, is a good example of the Eastlake style. Notice the incised carving around the top of the mirror and bed. A set like this illustrates the Victorians' love of matched pieces of furniture.

claw foot sofa or a 1770s Queen Anne highboy might stand in the parlor by a Rococo Revival chair or an Eastlake marble-topped table. There may also have been a piece in another big look of the Victorian era. This one marked the return of spooky furniture.

As machinery was advancing to a more high-tech stage, furniture manufacturers looked for new gimmicks to sell more pieces. Car makers do the same thing when they change their models each year. This marketing strategy made the industrialists look backwards long before the advent of modern furniture.

Photograph courtesy of Skinner, Inc.

This Renaissance Revival walnut bookcase from the late 1800s with all its intricate carving really shows how this style could also be called "Medieval Revival" style and how similar it is to furniture called the Aesthetic Movement.

Photograph courtesy of Skinner, Inc.

These slipper chairs date from about 1875-1885. Their frames are either oak or walnut which have been "ebonized" to make them look like they were crafted from costly black wood.

They rediscovered spooky furniture.

Homemakers in the 1860s were ripe for these ancient styles from the 1500s and 1600s. Their ornateness catered to the Victorian ideas of refinement. This trend christened the Renaissance Revival style. Its time of chicness was from about 1860 to as late as 1890.

Loomism: Think of Renaissance Revival as Medieval Revival to understand its visual impact. This marked the return of spooky furniture. Carvings of cherubs, lion's heads, winged animals, and other heavy duty motifs became valued.

Renaissance Revival furniture was perfect for upscale Victorian houses. Unlike 1700s ones, those mansions had high ceilings, tall, skinny windows, and varnished woodwork. All that created a dark ambiance. The record of woodwork and wall paneling being painted or left in its original state is very intriguing. Until the early 1700s, oak or walnut woodwork in swanky residences was usually varnished like furniture. That shadowy background proved to be ideal for the somber furniture of the Tudor and Jacobean era.

By the early 1700s, decorating in both Britain and the Colonies followed the Queen Anne style. Everything lightened up. As furnishings became more cheerful, so did woodwork. Paneled walls were painted gray, white, or other colors to compliment the scheme of a room. In existing homes the woodwork often got a facelift by paint. In new ones, pine or another inexpensive wood got a similar treatment. Penny pinching is an antique habit. It made no sense to use fine lumber that would be hidden. At George and Martha's Mount Vernon, the walls in the foyer are pine which were grained-painted to resemble costlier mahogany. The rest of their interior catered to 1700s tendency for painted woodwork.

Painted woodwork was popular in the United States roughly the same time as understatement ruled decorating tastes about 1700 through 1840.

Around 1840 at the beginning of the Victorian era, the interiors of houses grew darker. Woodwork was left in its natural colors. Walnut and oak were mostly used. Rooms grew drearier, and only somber colors such as rose, gold, and deep greens were chosen. So you can see the setting was perfect for the return of spooky furniture.

Rococo Revival pieces could be massive, but their curvy fronts and cabriole legs helped retain a certain lightness. Renaissance/Medieval Revival was taller, more massive, and even more ornate.

Sideboards and beds soaring almost as high as churches were as equally elaborate. Walnut was the first choice, and mahogany was suddenly again in demand. Pieces were made in factories in either Grand Rapids, Michigan, or Cincinnati, Ohio, and shipped all over the country. Decoration included flowers, fruit, scrolls, and even busts of Neoclassical ladies resembling the Statue of Liberty. In furniture terms, the Statue of Liberty, a gift from France to celebrate our Centennial, is a Renaissance Revival statue. Even water goblets were created in this motif. A Pittsburgh glass maker, Duncan Miller, made glassware using the "Three Faces of Eve" pattern. This had a woman's face in three sides of the stem of goblets or compotes.

The motif recalling the world's most famous statue is, in furniture terms, pure Renaissance Revival style.

The sideboard is the definitive example of the Renaissance Revival style. It can be anywhere from six to nine feet high. The bottom contains storage areas with doors, drawers for flatware, and a marble surface. The top is a vertical piece that usually frames a mirror. Decorations sometimes included, near its peak, a fully dimensionally carved deer or elk head complete with detailed horns. This artistic eeriness appealed to many Victorians as the zenith of good taste.

Now you can fully understand how regarding this style as Renaissance/Medieval Revival makes it easier to fathom.

Renaissance Revival furnishings were quality mass-produced pieces for middle- and upper-middle-class homes. After a while handmade versions of this style emerged. In the past ten years or so, the Aesthetic Movement, a new designation, has come into antiques. This name was coined by museum curators and others to define Renaissance/Medieval Revival furniture that was not mass-produced but individually crafted.

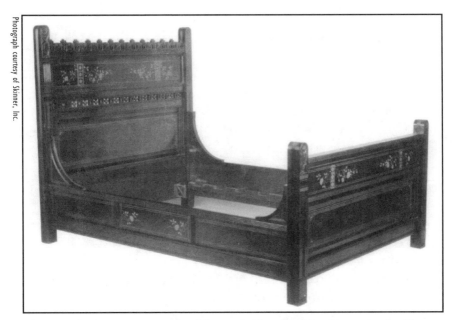

Photograph courtesy of Skinner, Inc.

This Aesthetic Movement bed from the late 1800s almost looks like an Eastlake style piece except this one was more expensive and handmade.

Photograph courtesy of Skinner, Inc.

An American ladies writing desk in cherry from 1885 is Aesthetic Movement with a touch of Oriental look especially in its carving on the drawer fronts.

As machinery took over more and more in the late 1800s, many artisans were not pleased. The Arts and Crafts Movement starting at that time wanted more handmade articles. The Aesthetic Movement followed the Arts and Crafts handmade ideology. It created handmade renditions following Renaissance/Medieval Revival trademarks.

An exhibition in the 1980s by the Metropolitan Museum of Art in New York City really gave the Aesthetic Movement clout. "In Pursuit of Beauty" highlighted gems by such cabinet makers as the Herter Brothers of New York, and other 1870s and 1880s makers. The pieces, although handmade, were like Renaissance/Medieval Revival: massive and ornate. Of course, there was lots of spooky carving.

Do you know who really sets the trends in antiques? Who can elevate the status of articles from garage-sale level to those two magical words for an antique—museum quality? Wonderful museum curators have this power. As they pick items for their exhibitions, they unknowingly endorse and elevate items to museum quality.

An Aesthetic Movement writing table before that show was considered nothing out of the ordinary. Then suddenly it jumped into the big leagues—right up there with Chippendale pieces. A museum endorsement creates trendiness and prices go

Photograph courtesy of Skinner, Inc.

This Wedgwood Jug was made in 1874 to be an official souvenir of the American Centennial in Philadelphia in 1876. It was during this time Americans became interested in the styles popular during America's Colonial period. The "Centennial" term was coined for reproduction of the Queen Anne, Chippendale, Hepplewhite, Sheraton, and Empire pieces.

up, which is what happened to Aesthetic Movement furnishings.

So you can see the Victorian era was cluttered with many styles: Rococo Revival, Eastlake, Renaissance/Medieval Revival, and more to boot.

To celebrate America's one hundredth birthday in 1876, the Centennial (something like a World's Fair) was held in

Photograph courtesy of Skinner, Inc.

This 1885 scene by Frank Henry Shapleigh (American 1842-1906) "The Old Kitchen In Bartlett, New Hampshire" reveals in art what Centennial pieces are. They glorify America's Colonial past with its Windsor and ladder back chairs and pewter as depicted by the artist.

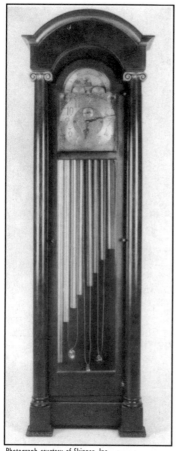

Photograph courtesy of Skinner, Inc.

Long before the Centennial era, grandfather clocks were simply called "long case clocks" because of their tall cabinets. During the Centennial era a popular song referred to this type as "my grandfather clock" and the term has happily stuck. This late 1880s model captures the Empire style with its columns on either side of the glass door.

Philadelphia. This exhibition glorified everything American and had lasting results. Suddenly America realized it had a past. It is like turning thirty and sensing awareness of a background. The late 1870s was when genealogy got going and Americans fell in love with antiques. To cater to this new awareness of antiques, those furniture makers who copied Medieval designs looked at American pieces from the 1700s and 1600s for ideas.

The result marked the beginning of the great business of furniture reproductions. Soon Grand Rapids and Cincinnati, already synonymous for fine quality machine-made furniture, made many reproductions. Just as their ancestors, Americans fell in love with the Queen Anne, Chippendale,

Photographs courtesy of Skinner, Inc.

These two photos illustrate the flamboyance of a Centennial copy versus the real McCoy. The English (doesn't matter if it is English or American) Centennial chairs are slightly too robust looking, especially in the carvings in the upper corners when compared to an American chair from the 1700s.

Heppleton (Sheraton and Hepplewhite), and Empire styles.

The copies from the late 1870s or early 1880s are called Centennial because they date from America's birthday celebration. Those 1870s or 1880s models were made differently. They have glued-on carving indicating factory origin as opposed to the 1700s handcarving out of solid piece of wood.

How can we tell the difference between a Centennial chair and "one of the period," meaning the real McCoy? It is easier than ever expected. During the height of Victorian love for ornateness, overstatement dominated, whether in clothes such as those caboose-styled bustles on women's dresses or the overly elaborate carving on a chair. In order to sell furniture, makers of Centennial pieces catered to this highly strung decorating mentality. Thus, those copies of the pre-1840 styles lacked the balance and understatement of the originals.

Centennial pieces are too flamboyant to be accurate reproductions. This was the "Gilded Age" to quote Mr. Twain. We can also think of it as the "Mother of Pearl Era." How Victorians loved using the lining of sea shells to decorate things.

There are other splashy traits distinguishing Centennial copies from the originals. Sometimes makers made the chair backs taller (remember the Victorian love of high ceilings) than those on Chippendale chairs. The decoration on the younger ones was just too grandiose for the staid tastes of the previous century. However, Wallace Nutting (1861-1941) made authentic reproductions. His pieces are highly collected and have become pricey. The popularity of Centennial pieces had long-range impact in the early days of the twentieth century, but that is another antiques story.

In the 1890s, the last decade of the reign of Queen Victoria, the most razmatazz of all the styles was born. Before discovering that, credit must be given where credit is due. Acclaim must be given to the number one, universally adored antique chair.

21

The Windsor Chair:
The All-time Favorite Chair

Whether your favorite chair is a Morris, the one with wings, or a curly Rococo Revival rendition, you will probably love one other type. This one goes with all decors, time periods, and even looks great by the computer: the Windsor chair.

Can you believe this type of chair has been made continuously for more than 270 years? The style originated in England between 1710 and 1720 near Windsor Castle. Hence they came to be called Windsor chairs. By the 1720s they became "urban" and were being made in London. Yankees started creating these beauties in the 1740s. English Windsors usually had a solid splat in the central back section while American versions had upright spindles all around the back.

Photograph courtesy of Skinner, Inc.

The parts of Windsor chairs were made of various woods. Seats were pine while legs and backs were often maple or oak. Because they were a mixture of woods, they were usually painted dark green or yellow. This

Here is a mid 1700s English version of the Windsor chair which many brand as the coziest chair ever made.

Photograph courtesy of Skinner, Inc.

Here are two later British Windsor chairs made in the 1830s before the reign of Victoria, during the days of her uncle Bill, William IV.

made them appear to be crafted from the same wood. Those two happy colors added to their appeal because they brightened many a dreary interior.

Francis Trumble, a Philadelphia cabinet maker, made 114 Windsors for the Philadelphia State House. Before Benjamin Franklin, Robert Morris, and others signed the Declaration of Independence at Independence Hall, they got up from Windsor chairs. George and Martha had a set on the front veranda so guests could sit and view the Potomac River flowing in front of Mt. Vernon. When you visit their home today, feel like 1700s gentry as you sit upon reproductions of their Windsors.

Windsors have been constructed nonstop since their invention and served many uses. They were usually seen in the kitchen, guest room, or in the garden. Painting them green was

Photograph courtesy of Skinner, Inc.

so popular because it "matched the outside." Whatever color, solid splat or spindle back, they are always in fashion.

That country look of Windsor can be deceiving. They were one of the first chairs to be created by the factory system and they played an important part in the Industrial Revolution. Eli Whitney

A 1700s Yankee version of the famous chair.

Photograph courtesy of Skinner, Inc.

These two date from the early 1800s and still have some of their original black paint.

developed a machine to stamp out identical parts for muskets in 1798 which eventually ended handcraftsmanship for guns. His idea of interchangeable parts really gave a boost to mass production, and by 1808 clocksmith Eli Terry and chair maker Lambert Hitchcock mass-produced their goods.

By then Windsor chairs had become an important part of the machine age. In Connecticut, Windsors were factory made, and parts were produced in large quantities. Soon they became standardized and interchangeable. This was an early example of assembly-line production. A cabinet maker bought ready-made parts and then assembled and painted them.

Photograph courtesy of Skinner, Inc.

These early mass produced chairs date from the 1810 to 1840 and are very similar to the ones in the Kauffmans' kitchen at Fallingwater.

Different styles of chairs come and go in demand, but not the Windsor. What is the secret behind its eternal worship? Even the Victorians, with their preference for plush and ornateness, loved them. We shall let our bodies do the explaining. Just plop yourself down in one. Now you realize there is no puzzle to their appeal, they are wonderfully c-o-m-f-o-r-t-a-b-l-e.

Here is one more pleasing morsel about those alluring antiques. Can you believe that a summer house designed by ultra modern architect, Frank Lloyd Wright, would have Windsors? Mr. Wright usually engineered most of the furnishings for his works but not in this residence.

You can tour the magical Fallingwater, located south of Pittsburgh, and see for yourself. In the Kaufmann's sleek kitchen, you naturally expect chrome stools. Those predictably would have been Mr. Wright's choice because they would befit that very high-tech kitchen. Clustered around the kitchen table instead are 1830s versions of the same type of chairs that George and Martha had on the front porch of Mount Vernon. Mrs. Kaufmann, besides having superb taste in houses, knew the chairs' merit. That is probably the best endorsement ever for Windsor chairs!

Naive (Folk) Art and Country Furniture

Learning about Folk Art could be tough—but not for us. It will be easy and fun. By now, perhaps, you have become self-confident Group II Collectors. We like what appeals to us without the slightest concern about an antique's breeding. It simply does not matter. That is one attractive feature of Folk Art. There are no guidelines to define it. All that looseness could make it intimidating for the less secure, but there is nothing perplexing about its appeal. Folk Art is a highly individualistic and informal art for both its creator and the collector.

In trying to describe antique folk art, experts used to say that antiques with a rustic or country look were primitives. That word implies a lack of quality and shows a downright uppity attitude. Fortunately today, the word primitive is avoided.

The best way to define Folk Art is: any handmade object created by an untrained or informally trained artisan. That is it.

The one universal trait folk artists of all eras and all nationalities share is their lack of formal training. They did not go to art school to study portraiture or apprentice with a cabinet maker. A folk artist could have been a girl stitching a sampler during the Civil War or a vagabond trading carvings for food in the 1930s.

Folk Art pieces that predate 1910 are generally considered antique. A later item such as a 1930s wood carving is a semi-antique. Folk art being made today is, of course, an example of future antiques.

Photograph courtesy of Skinner, Inc.

Besides Mrs. Rockefeller and Mrs. Webb, we antiquers owe much to Anna Mayr Robertson (American, 1860-1961) better known as Grandma Moses. This lady whose art was discovered when she was 78 years old, really made Naive Art fashionable.

When collecting antique Folk Art, remember what one person considers Folk Art another may call junk. Urban antiques can usually be classified in a specific era or style to establish their pedigrees. No such regulations exist for what is considered Folk Art.

Be prepared to be a nonconformist for this unique field of antiques. Wear your suit of armor to protect your sensitivity. You may sometimes hear, "Oh my, it is lovely," but be prepared for remarks like, "Why do you want that old thing?"

It is a real power trip to collect Folk Art. We alone are the judge of what is appealing. You decide whether a quilt, a sampler, or an almost flat-looking painting of a boy and his puppy is quality.

Collectors owe a great deal to two fantastic antiquers. These two were trail blazers for getting Folk Art appreciated. It is fascinating that both ladies were wealthy and could afford almost any costly, museum-quality antique. However, they are models for the Group II antiquers. These pioneers collected what pleased them rather than what was well-liked or in pristine condition.

Abby Aldrich Rockefeller (1874-1948) was married to John D. Rockefeller, Jr., the Standard Oil heir. With all that money, you would think her life was antiques heaven. It was not true. Her husband constantly voiced his disapproval of her selections. Mr. R. was a Group I Collector with very conservative tastes, typical of that clique. His choices tended to be pedigreed such as French tapestries from the Middle Ages. Do not get the wrong impression; he was a wonderful guy. He gave millions for the restoration of Williamsburg, Virginia, and the Palace of Versailles in France. However, he and his wife constantly were at odds about the antiques each collected.

Bernice Kert in her splendid book, *Abby Aldrich Rockefeller the Woman in the Family,* details the conflicts that exist when a Group I and a Group II collector are husband and wife. Mrs. R., so unique for back then, eagerly sought Folk Art antiques. Today tourists visiting charming eighteenth-century Williamsburg can also visit the Rockefeller home, Bassett Hall. Her collection of weather vanes, chalk ware, and samplers are beautifully displayed.

Mrs. R. did not limit her artistic endeavors just to Folk Art. This terrific lady was one of the founders of the Museum of Modern Art in New York City. That was pretty daring for the late 1930s. Most critics then thought Modern Art and Folk Art belonged in the same place—the city dump.

Our second great antiquer, Electra Havemeyer Webb (1888-1960) was the daughter of Louisine and Harry Havemeyer. Her parents were famous New York collectors who purchased the works of Impressionistic artists.

Did Electra trek in her parents' aesthetic footsteps when collecting? With the unusual name of Electra, it seems perfectly logical that she would follow the beat of her own drummer for collecting. By the time she was eighteen, Electra was hooked on American antiques. She had little interest in fancy urban ones such as silver tea services by Paul Revere. She collected, or

Photograph courtesy of Skinner, Inc.

These wooden gates from a fence dating from the mid 1800s are a form of Naive Art.

rather stockpiled, items that were considered rubbish, namely American Folk Art. Her first major purchase was a cigar store Indian, a relic from the nineteenth century that had originally been used as an advertising sign for a tobacco shop.

History records that Mrs. Havemeyer, whose tastes were undoubtedly similar to Mr. Rockefeller's, was absolutely disgusted with her daughter's choices. Generations of Folk Art collectors are in Mrs. Webb's debt. In 1947 she created the Shelburne Museum in Shelburne, Vermont, a tremendous resource for Folk Art.

Photograph courtesy of Skinner, Inc.

The possibilities in this field of antiques are limitless. Here is a violin case that was decorated by its owner in the late 1800s.

A very good but informally trained artist did this banner depicting Lincoln some time after the Civil War.

Photograph courtesy of Skinner, Inc.

Mrs. Webb's and Mrs. Rockefeller's enthusiasm marked the beginning of Folk Art losing its secondhand status. Now it has acquired those two very expensive words when it comes to antiques: museum quality.

Shortly before Mrs. Webb died, someone asked her how she defined Folk Art. Her reply: "Folk means people which includes all of us. Therefore Folk Art is the self-expression of art from the heart and hands of the people." To this day no one has ever better or more lovingly explained Folk Art.

Let us follow the caring examples of Mrs. Webb and Mrs. Rockefeller. We should call these antiques by the name the Brits and French use. They more accurately and graciously call it Naive Art. Artifacts from the people have a casual and straight-forward beauty.

There is much encouraging news when it comes to shopping for Naive Art. Even though it is finally respected and much of it is in museums, there are still good deals available. How could that be? There are no formal defini-tions, so self-confidence is needed by the collector. That could be fearful for some except for those who follow Mrs. Webb's and Mrs. R.'s example.

Perhaps quilts are the best expression of Naive Art. They have become pretty fashionable, but there are still many

Photograph courtesy of Skinner, Inc.

Quilts, such as this 1800s American beauty with its plume and star design, are a prime example of fashionable and affordable Naive Art.

affordable ones. Another good choice is hooked rugs, especially those depicting dogs or cats. American samplers are expensive, so why not find an English or French one that typically sells for much less?

A few years ago in Paris, on the same trip that we bought all those antique prints, Pete and Dianne went to the Rodin Museum while I went antiquing. Upon entering a tiny shop filled with everything from French china to paintings, something yelled at me. There it was on the floor in a corner. A sampler dated 1867 with cheerful colors highlighted a mother, her children, and their dog. The original frame even had wavy, handmade glass. It was a steal (after negotiation, of course) at $350. A similar American one would be double or triple that price. Do not overlook Naive Art from other countries. It can often be less exorbitant than the Yankee version.

Photograph courtesy of Skinner, Inc.

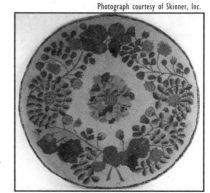

This yarn-sewn floral design from the 1800s is a charming example of Naive Art.

Photograph courtesy of Skinner, Inc.

To label these two charming portraits from circa 1830-1850 as "primitive" or "Folk" art is an injustice.

Naive paintings are works that have been made with paint, pencil, ink, pastel, watercolor, or chalk applied to a flat surface. It can be board, canvas, or even the door of a cabinet. Paintings have become the costliest category of Naive Art. Scenes of children with a beloved pet are the most cherished. Paintings by Ammi Phillips (1788-1865) appearing almost one-dimensional have sold for more than $250,000. That is not bad for a self-taught artist whose work was labeled "primitive." Bravo, Mr. Phillips!

Sculpture includes three-dimensional objects made from clay or wood. Eagles such as Mrs. R.'s and cigar store Indians such as Mrs. W.'s are now highly collected. Other mediums

Photograph courtesy of Skinner, Inc.

Carved American eagles, such as this one, particularly pleased Mrs. Rockefeller.

Photograph courtesy of Skinner, Inc.

This swan decoy painted by John T. Newark of North Carolina captures the elegance of the bird.

were often clay, stone, and metal. Even marble was used for everything from decoys, ship figureheads, weather vanes, to tombstones.

Country furniture is an important segment of Naive Art. Since we prefer the term Naive Art, regard this antique as Naive Furniture. Folk Art is cliché and sets up images of hearts and ducks.

To be truly Naive, a chair or table should have been individually made by an informally trained artisan. It is natural to confuse country with urban furniture. Here is an easy way to distinguish between the two. Think of a carpenter constructing a cupboard and a city cabinet maker creating a similar piece. A carpenter is very capable but less formally taught in furniture design and other aspects than his urban counterpart.

Naive furniture has certain traits. Pieces were primarily utilitarian, made for a particular need such as a plate rack. Fabrication usually took place at home by hand using local woods such as cherry, birch, pine, or others.

There is a simplicity of design. Naive items rarely follow any certain style. If a Queen Anne piece were made rurally, it would usually be in a less-detailed version. There would be rounded, straight legs rather than cabriole as we discovered about country Queen Anne furniture. There would be little if any carving because that required formal training. Veneer is almost never seen on Naive pieces. Planks are usually at least one inch thick and are not the same width. Timber probably was cut in the artisan's yard, not from a lumber yard.

Photograph courtesy of Skinner, Inc.

The corner cupboard is perhaps the number one piece of Naive Furniture. These two from the American South date from the mid 1800s and follow no definite style. Yet, both are highly collected antiques.

Country cabinets were often decorated with exuberant colors. Yellow was a popular choice to brighten a drab room. Pine sometimes would be decorated with a graining technique to resemble fancier oak or mahogany or to make an item appear from only one wood.

Those inventive rural people never let anything go to waste. A paint formula included milk mixed with any leftovers. Eggs, coffee, and the blood of butchered animals were used. Barns were red because animal blood was the most plentiful ingredient. Also, that color was practically neon-like during a blizzard. In the late 1860s as the Industrial Revolution progressed, ready-made paints became available which ultimately ended the demand for milk paint.

Photograph courtesy of Skinner, Inc.

This painted secretary desk is a true example of Naive furniture. From Western New York state and dating from about 1830, the desk follows no specific furniture style.

Antiques dealer Marilyn Haley, known for her country antiques, says: "It is often difficult to tell urban from country." She warns to be careful of pieces that have had their veneer removed exposing the pine. This is often done to 1840s machine-made Late Empire pieces to give them that country look. Remember to buy reputable retail. Get authenticity verified on your receipt, and enjoy.

The effects of the Industrial Revolution arrived at the farmhouse in the form of catalogues delivered by the U.S. Post Office. Sears, Roebuck and Montgomery Ward offered mass-produced tables, chairs, and other pieces cheaper than homemade versions. Those two merchants nearly ended Naive Furniture production. By 1900 Naive Furniture was rarely made.

Today, renditions command high prices. Naive Art antiques are part of Americana, which would please Mrs. Rockefeller and Mrs. Webb.

23

Dishes or China?

In the old days when one referred to the ceramic used for dining utensils as china rather than dishes, it was considered well bred. No one cared about technicalities, only gentility. Gram never took her grandson to the dish department at that great Chicago emporium, Marshall Field's. Rather we went to the china department. We are about to unravel how the alluring term, china, is one of the great misnomers of all time. The correct label for what pasta is served upon is about to become as clear as an antique glass goblet.

Those wise Greeks did not worry about correct slogans. Anything made from clay was called ceramic. Taking that natural resource and making it into a bowl or plate has remained basically the same throughout the centuries.

There are many categories of ceramics. They all have clay and are similarly made. The potter kneads wet clay to remove air bubbles. Then it is shaped into various items by one or two methods. Throwing it on a potter's wheel (which gave our friend Mr. Wedgwood such trouble) is the first method. The second involves putting liquid-like clay into a mold. Then the newly shaped object, created by either method, is fired (baked) until hard. This stage is called "cheese." Decoration can be hand painted or done by a decal-type process called transfer. Glazing, the final stage, applies a glass-like coating over the ceramic to protect the decoration and make it usable. Then it is fired in a kiln (oven) to dry.

A punch bowl from China in the "Rose Mandarin" pattern dates from the 1800s and is famous for its rose color.

Photograph courtesy of Skinner, Inc.

Clay is a malleable soil coming from decaying rocks and is primarily aluminum silicate. Different types are used for various ceramics. The kind, how long, and at what temperature it is fired, determines the type. Kaolin is a very white clay and necessary for porcelain. It remains that color after firing. First found in China, deposits were discovered later in Germany, England, and the United States.

Porcelain is the perfect place to begin our study of ceramics. The debate between saying "china" or "dishes" dates long before Gram or most of our ancestors.

Westerners truly have a passion for porcelain. This love began when a famous Italian toured China. That country was unknown to Europeans until Marco Polo (1254-1324). In the late 1200s he brought home to Venice some Chinese novelties including toilet tissue, gunpowder, and porcelain.

Compared to the Chinese, Europeans were pretty backwards, and they had nothing like porcelain. Europeans considered this white, cold-to-the-touch, and unscratchable ceramic to be a marvel. At that time European ceramics were chunky, thick dishes. This newly arrived crockery was not called by its correct name, porcelain. Rather it was called china after its homeland. This mistake was never corrected. Fancy soup bowls, teacups, and other banqueting apparatus continued to be labeled china. Anyone considered even remotely civilized never used the term dishes. No one cared that dishes is the more precise designation which includes all types of ceramics whether earthenware or porcelain.

Photograph courtesy of Skinner, Inc.

Nanking porcelain from the Chinese city of Nanking is famous for its blue and white pattern resembling the English blue "Willow" design.

During these days of throw-away plastic, that old-fashioned expression sounds especially picturesque. Here is to our beloved family members who preferred the word china.

The term porcelain comes from French or Italian, meaning cowrie shell. Porcelain lives up to its name. Unlike opaque and heavier pottery, it has a translucent and lightweight body. When you hold a porcelain teacup to the light, it shines through the bottom.

Porcelain was made in China as early as 960 A.D. Undecorated white porcelain, Blanc-de-Chine, means Chinese White. Various color combinations were made. Blue and white from the Chinese porcelain-making cities of Canton and Nanking were really popular. Pieces from the late 1700s and 1800s crafted for export to Europe and America are known as "Chinese Export."

The Germans at Meissen in the Saxony region were the first Europeans to successfully produce porcelain. In 1709 the correct clay, kaolin, was found. Also artisans figured out that a high temperature for firing was needed. This porcelain is called Meissen or Dresden. Meissen refers to the town, and Dresden to the district. Figurines and candlesticks were decorated with flowers and cherubs following 1700s Rococo designs. Just as mid-1800s furniture (following the Victorian love for clutter) had much decoration, so did the Meissen and Dresden of this era. The logo for Meissen is crossed blue swords. Be careful

Photograph courtesy of Skinner, Inc.

These Meissen of Germany bowls in blue and white look like they were crafted in the 1700s but are really from the late 1800s.

when buying because there are many fakes. Buy reputable retail and get the guarantee of authenticity on your receipt.

The English also tried duplicating Chinese porcelain and finally succeeded in 1770 when kaolin was found in the Cornwall area. While other European ceramic makers received royal grants, the Brits perfected theirs under the free enterprise system. They never received any government financial backing. By 1842 seventeen British porcelain factories had been established including such stellar ones as Spode, Coalport, Wedgwood, and Worcester. It is reassuring that these distinguished names are alive and booming. What they make today are future antiques.

About 1800 the English added ground bone ash from farm animals to the wet kaolin clay, producing bone china. Notice the more precise term, bone porcelain, was not chosen. No one dared to change tradition, so technically incorrect but cultivated-sounding bone china became the name. It is more lightweight and translucent than regular porcelain. It is always

Photograph courtesy of Skinner, Inc.

A very popular Spode blue transfer design from the mid 1800s depicts "Rebecca at the Well."

Photograph courtesy of Skinner, Inc.

A French Sevres plate from the 1700s is very Rococo in its floral and gold design.

the mark of quality, and just like Gram said, it does not chip as easily as nonbone china ceramics.

The French started making porcelain in 1673. Experts consider Sevres, founded by Louis XV near Paris, to be one of the finest porcelains ever crafted. Its ornate pieces from the 1700s were the height of Rococo style, and the mid-1800s ones followed Rococo Revival's lavishness. Sevres has always been upscale. In the late 1800s huge porcelain urns in deep blue with much gold decoration graced mantels in many American mansions.

Middle Americans in the 1800s also loved French china from another area. Limoges, a city in Southern France, the

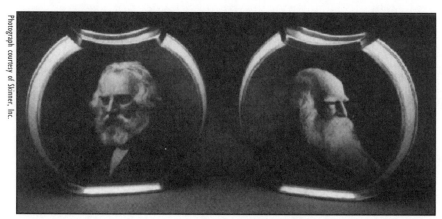

Photograph courtesy of Skinner, Inc.

The factories located in Limoges, France, besides being famous for sets of china, also created fine decorative pieces such as this circa 1885 pair of porcelain vases with portraits of Longfellow and W. Cullen Bryant. Just like the Brits, the French made items expressly for the Yankees.

hometown of artist Pierre Renoir (1841-1919) had rich kaolin deposits, so many porcelain factories started there. The most famous is Haviland founded by ex-Yankee David Haviland. He started making china in the 1840s to export to the United States. By 1900 Limoges was to French china what Detroit became to American automobiles. Homemakers did not say "Bring out the good china," but rather "Use the Limoges." That cherished word, Limoges, explained it all: mass-produced, affordable, and yet quality china. Today that attachment continues as those pieces are now venerated antiques. Haviland was the most famous, but other fine makers include Elite, T.V. Brand, and Arnfeldt. Many of these firms are still creating sets that will be future antiques.

Here is one more pinch of information about French china. When the famous Renoir was fourteen, he was apprenticed in Paris as a china decorator. He was so good that it led him from painting on china to canvas. A piece of Limoges by the great Renoir himself would really be a find.

Another peek at the what ceramics Europeans used before Mr. Polo's introduction of porcelain is enlightening. The few who could afford them had earthenware dishes. That is the oldest form of ceramics and is made from a nonwhite clay. Earthenware is thicker and not as translucent as porcelain. Firing it at a lower temperature renders it very porous, so glazing is needed to seal it. This prevents liquid from soaking through it and protects decoration.

While some European potters were trying to make porcelain, others were improving their earthenware. The ceramic business was one of the first to benefit from the technological advances of the Industrial Revolution.

The English were the earliest to turn out large amounts of quality ceramics. Before 1750, all decoration was handpainted. Liverpool, England, famous for the Beatles, is also important to collectors. China decorators there, Sadler and Green, invented transfer printing. This is a process similar to using decals. A scene that would be on a plate was first engraved upon a copper sheet. Then it was inked and the design printed upon a tissue-type paper. Water was applied to the paper, and the paper was

Photograph courtesy of Skinner, Inc.

This luncheon service by Podmore Walker and Co., a Staffordshire Pottery, dates from about the time of Rococo Revival. Its transfer design is in brown with a green border.

carefully laid upon the unglazed piece. The inked design transferred like a decal to the object, and the wet paper dissolved.

Transfer printing modernized the ceramic business. Handpainting was no longer the only way to embellish ceramics. This new way speeded up production resulting in reduced costs and increased quantities. The Brits, thanks to their ingenuity, became to ceramics what the Japanese are now to electronics. It put the Staffordshire region (about two and one-half hours north of London) on the antiques map for ceramics.

Transfer printing used various colors, but blue and white proved the most magnetic. The Brits finally succeeded at what the Chinese had done so well. They duplicated that sparkling duo which reminds us of white clouds on a sunny blue sky.

That team was so successful that today "Staffordshire" is a generic term meaning English earthenware with blue and white designs usually depicting historical scenes. A particularly charismatic subject highlighted the Marquis de Lafayette. In 1826 the former assistant to General Washington during the American Revolution visited the United States. British china makers cashed in on this by making souvenir plates or

Photograph courtesy of Skinner, Inc.

Perhaps the most famous blue and white duo in antiques history is the Staffordshire. This pair of compotes by English Joseph Stubbs showing the Boston State House dates from about 1825 to 1850.

pitchers depicting his tour. It is humorous that they were glorifying the French Lafayette, former enemy of Britain. "Business is business," thought those Brits. Here is another antique example of global economies. Today those plates are mighty pricey. Just be a Group II collector and find some affordable ones with problems and remember to hang them high.

Another example of blue and white needs to be applauded. Antique hats off to Holland, a stronghold of religious freedom, tulips, appreciation of pets, and, of course, those cabriole legs. We antiquers owe thanks to the pottery makers in the city of Delft. In the late 1600s they were the first Europeans to

Photograph courtesy of Skinner, Inc.

These blue and white Dutch plates from the city of Delft are an early successful example of Europeans capturing that magical blue and white combination popularized by the Chinese.

Photograph courtesy of Skinner, Inc.

Here is a real Ironstone China service possibly done by Mason's. Although English, its transfer design looks very Oriental.

duplicate on earthenware that special look started by the Chinese. Today Delft, another antiques generic term, is synonymous for glorious blue and white Dutch ceramics.

Another famous member of the earthenware family is ironstone. In 1797 Miles Mason established a factory in Staffordshire for ironstone. Because it was heavy, durable, and economical, it became the Corningware of the 1800s. Rarely used in grand homes, it added charm to cottages, bungalows, and farmhouses. It became so successful that by 1813 Mr. Mason's son, Charles, finally took out a patent.

Their mark read: "Mason's Patent Ironstone China." Those smart Masons did not worry over semantics but realized the clout of using the word china. Mason's Ironstone is a beloved antique and is still made in Staffordshire, now owned by Wedgwood. A client recently told me that hers is even microwavable—quite a testimony to its practicality. Other renowned makers include Johnson Brothers, Meakin, Adams, and Alcock. These firms used various names such as stoneware, stone china, pearl ware, and others. Ironstone China remains the most used term.

The best treasured design on earthenware is, of course, the Willow pattern. It was a Western invention like chop suey. The first really traditional Willow pattern was originated by Josiah Spode around 1810. It was English trying to look Chinese. The

Photograph courtesy of Skinner, Inc.

These pieces from circa 1880 were made by the Pennsylvania firm, Morley, Griffen, Smith, and Hill Potteries in a famous Majolica pattern called "Shell and Seaweed."

transfer design consisted of a willow tree, two pagodas, two birds, and three people crossing a bridge. The Brits, Yankees, and even the Japanese have produced the Willow pattern. It came in many colors, but as you know, the blue and white is the all-time favorite.

A very trendy ceramic due to its plugs in decorating magazines is Majolica. This pottery with colorful designs really compliments pine furniture. Majolica, a generic name, designates thick earthenware with a heavy glaze and brightly colored almost three-dimensional raised designs. It originated in the 1300s on the island of Majolica off the cost of Spain. The Italians spotted it and started making it in the 1400s. Patterns depict cabbage, fruits, ferns, and even asparagus. By the late 1800s it was made in France, Germany, and England. Wedgwood, Minton, and George Jones are the best known English ones. The firm of George Morely, Griffen, Smith, and Hill in the late 1800s made American versions.

How do you tell the age of a ceramic? Turn it over and read the label. Those marvelous Brits have marked theirs the clearest. English pieces make a great foundation for learning about ceramics. Once you quickly master theirs, you are ready to tackle your other favorite countries' ceramics.

Many older ceramics are unmarked. If a teacup has nothing, that could indicate age or youth. It could be modern and lost its paper label, or it could be old dating before 1891. What happened that year? The McKinley Tariff Act went into force. This law intended to protect American industries. It declared that for a foreign item to enter the United States, it had to be marked with its country of origin. A Willow plate made by Royal Doulton before 1891 only had the Doulton logo. After 1891 "England" had to be included. That helps date the plate between 1891 and the World War I era. Around 1918 "Made in" was added to the "England" part.

Twentieth-century china gets easier to pinpoint. The more information, the newer it is. If it says "acid resisting colours," that indicates the 1930s. "Dishwasher safe" is probably from the 1950s, and "microwavable" means yesterday. Here is the label from a brand-new plate; "Since 1883 Johnson Brothers has been making fine tableware for over 100 years, establishing a proud reputation for craftsmanship and quality of designs. Old British Castles copyright Johnson Brothers 1929, made in England." Remember the more information, the younger the item. That is also true for other antiques. Like any generalization, there are exceptions, but this guide should help more often than fail.

Here are two more ways for determining age. The transfer design on the "British Castles" plate is as precise as an etching on paper. The decoration on an earlier one, 1930s "Vista" by Mason's, is not as clear-cut. A third, marked only with "Ridgway's," indicates pre-1891 production. The 1800s ones are smudgy compared to the others. That seems a defect but not necessarily so. It is a type of ceramic that many antiquers covet.

Ironstone decorated with blurred designs in blue upon a white background is called Flow Blue. When the transfer was done, the ink was allowed to flow or smudge. Around 1825 many Staffordshire potteries, such as Adams, Wedgwood, Alcock, and Ridgway's started making it. Neoclassical motifs such as large urns following the Empire style were popular. In the 1860s, views with flowers or cherubs were done in the

Photograph courtesy of Skinner, Inc.

This set is by Royal Crown Derby, founded about 1750 in the Derby region of England. It dates from the early 1800s and has the Neoclassical forms such as its urn shaped creamer. This service would look perfect placed on a Hepplewhite or Sheraton sideboard.

Rococo Revival style. Antique Flow Blue china is now very expensive. If it is your antique cup of tea, find affordable chipped versions. As a Group II collector, display them to show their best side.

Here is another aid in dating china. The Wedgwood Museum at the factory shows how china follows furniture styles. That is the reason this book concentrates heavily on furniture designs. Once you have them down pat, you are off to dating other antiques. Say you spot a Rococo Revival floral design on a teapot like those you recognize on the back of a Rococo Revival sofa. Now that you know furniture designs, you can accurately assume the china is from the 1850s or 1860s.

Here is the only reference book needed to date British china. Find it in the Art and Music Department of your public library. *The Encyclopedia for British Pottery and Porcelain Marks* by Geoffrey A. Godden (Crown Publishers) is an antiquer's best friend. Through the years this appraiser has worn out his copy.

Using it is fun, such as when I checked the dates on my family set. Gram gave me her most prized heirloom, her good set of china. It belonged to her beloved older sister, our great Aunt Nana. Its pieces were decorated with Oriental trees and flowers. It supposedly had been in her husband's family, Uncle Gerald's, "for over a hundred years." Its mark reads: "Indian Tree, Soho Pottery, Cobridge England." A dead giveaway to youthfulness is that the pattern's name is printed very simply. A label from the mid-1800s would be more flamboyantly printed in true Rococo Revival fashion. Gram's is very sedate. Also you noticed the word "England" is included. Well, Mr. Godden says Aunt Nana's china dates from 1906 to 1922. When it comes to age, family heirlooms tend to be exaggerated. How many times have you heard: "It belonged to Bill's great-grandmother, and she died in 1935 at the age of 90." So one assumes incorrectly that her porcelain tea service dates from around 1845, the year of her birth. It could have been a wedding present in 1865, or one for her fiftieth anniversary in 1915, or she could have bought it herself in 1934. Unlike movie stars' ages, family antiques tend to accumulate years.

At first, this collector was disappointed. Then the appraiser took over and said: "It is the quality and not the age that is important." Remember old is no guarantee for quality. Also keep in mind that age does not equal craftsmanship. Quality is the most desirable trait.

The competition between Japan, the United States, and Britain is really quite antique. These days the Japanese seem to

Photograph courtesy of Skinner, Inc.

These covered vases are Delftware from the 1700s. Modern version of these vases are still being produced today.

have the market cornered on high-tech equipment and automobiles. For years they have also been giving the Brits and Yankees tough contests in the china department. For more than a hundred years they have been making porcelain that was less costly and equal in quality to American and British. Sears and Ward's in the early 1900s sold Japanese goods. Vases with heavy gold ornamentation around a handpainted landscape are marked "Nippon." That is Japanese for Japan, and indicates the period of 1891 to about 1921. Recall how the McKinley ruling declared that country of origin was to be marked on all imports to the United States. Around 1921 our government said "Japan" should be used rather than "Nippon." In time, "made in" was added. Nippon china is probably one of today's best-selling antiques. It is quality and still affordable.

There are as many names for the various types of ceramics as there are patterns. You are now familiar with the main ones to go onward in your china know-how. Here is hoping you agree with our elders who used the word china. Who cares about technicalities? They were absolutely right to prefer "china" over the more correct porcelain, earthenware, or other designations. Gentility still dictates avoiding that very disparaging idiom out of respect to Mr. Polo and our beloved predecessors. Who would want to collect old dishes when there is antique china to be relished?

The next chapter highlights affordable antiques that happen to be the tablemates of china.

24

Antique Glass: Class Without Much Cash

Glass may rhyme with class, but it still is an affordable antique. Glass has been mass-produced since the mid-1800s which means there are plenty of sleepers.

The Egyptians who invented glass discovered that heating sand and other ingredients to over 2,500 degrees Fahrenheit, produced a liquid. While molten it could be shaped into items such as goblets, and when cooled it became brittle and unchangeable.

The basic ingredients of glass are silica (sand), soda, and lime. Sand melts to form the glass, soda acts as a flux to allow the glass to melt at a lower temperature, and lime is a stabilizer. Various oxides can be added to create different colors. Adding lead allows the glass, once cooled, to be cut and decorated without breaking in the process.

How a glass item is shaped is the key to its classification. The basic formula and handmade fabrication are basically the same since the days of the Pharaohs. The Romans were also good at glassmaking, and their descendants, the Venetians, continued this skill. Glassmaking in the hometown of Marco Polo has been going on since 1083, mainly on the island of Murano, not far from San Marco Cathedral.

By the 1500s Venetians were going full pace and guarded their glassmaking techniques. While Venice made household items, other Europeans created glorious stained-glass windows, such as those of Sainte Chappelle in Paris. Those colorful

Photograph courtesy of Skinner, Inc.

Not far from San Marco church in Venice is the island of Murano, where fine glass has been made for centuries.

windows depicting religious heroes must have literally brightened the lives of many worshipers.

In the early 1600s, secret formulas escaped Venice and went to the French. They have a history of borrowing artistic ideas from the Italians. Later the techniques arrived in England and Bohemia, two future important glass centers.

Competition from other areas in the 1600s caused Venetian glass to fall in sales. Then in the late 1800s Venice made a comeback. Today the most famous Venetian glassmaker, Murano, still located on that nearby island, is more popular than ever. Its handmade products are definitely antiques of the future.

The easiest way to learn about antique glass is to study how it is created. The manner used to shape glass objects is how we classify them. The ways are: blown glass, mold-blown glass, pressed, and molded glass.

Blown Glass

Just as its name says, blown glass is shaped by air blown from the lungs of a glassmaker. Glass is heated to a semiliquid consistency. The next step uses a blowing iron—a long, hollow pipe or tube. It is slightly flared at the end with a wooden mouthpiece to protect the lips. The pipe is dipped into a pot of molten glass, and a small amount of liquid glass, called gather, adheres to its end. By blowing through the tube, the artisan shapes the glass. By now it has cooled somewhat allowing it to be removed. Then it is rolled over a heavy metal or marble

Photograph courtesy of Skinner, Inc.

Light looking hand blown glass from Venice is famous the world over.
This Neoclassical looking set dates from the late 1800s.

surface, like preparing pastry dough on a cutting board. The
cooled glass will not stick, and the pipe is rolled back and forth
to flatten the bottom of the glass piece. Then the still semimolten
glass is attached to the pontil rod for final shaping by blowing.
The pontil mark on the bottom of blown pieces is like a circular
scar or a broken-off tip. It is the "belly button" where the glass
was attached to the rod. This mark was left as the glass was broken
from the pipe. In time this rough spot was smoothed down.

The blowing method has existed since ancient times, but the
Industrial Revolution created a novel twist to the process.

Mold-blown Glass

Mold-blown glass was invented in 1827 by an American
mechanic. This way took less time to shape than the total breath
approach. The glassmaker placed molten glass on the tip of the
rod. Then it is inserted into the mold that had two or three
hinged parts. Air is blown into the tube which causes the molten
glass to go to all sides of the form to get its shape. When the glass
cools, the form comes apart quickly.

The key to detecting mold-blown glass is easy. It has marks
like seams on the bases. When the decoration is created by the
mold, the outside is the reverse of the inside.

An 1840-1845 compote of pressed glass by Sandwich in the Princess feather Medallion and Basket of Flowers design.

Photograph courtesy of Skinner, Inc.

The mold-blown process drastically changed production methods. Instead of being individually made and decorated by cutting, etching, or engraving, this could be done in one motion. Speedier glassmaking resulted in greater abundance, and prices came tumbling down.

Pressed Glass

The final segment of glass history is pressed glass, a low-cost and quick way to make glass. Its abundance catered to the Victorian zest for much bric-a-brac. It was first made about 1827 in the towns of Cambridge and Sandwich, Massachusetts. No lungs were required because molten glass was pressed into a mold by a plunger, which speeded up glassmaking. Pieces were smooth on the inside regardless of how deep the pattern was on the outside, something like waffles made on an iron. It was most successful with dishes, bowls, and cup plates.

Cup plates, a smaller edition of a saucer, have an interesting story. Made between 1800 to 1850, those little treasures, three to four inches in diameter, were used to hold a teacup. People poured scalding tea or coffee into a saucer to cool before drinking it because teeth were usually in a delicate state. Then they sipped from the saucer which was deeper than modern ones. The cup, meanwhile, rested upon the cup plate to protect the table or cloth. Cup plates were made in large quantities mainly by the Boston and Sandwich Glass Company. That firm also made glass handles embellishing many 1830s chests of drawers.

The Sandwich firm tried to duplicate costlier cut glass. Something quite different but nevertheless charming resulted.

Photograph courtesy of Skinner, Inc.

Here is fine Bohemian glass from the late 1800s. The candlesticks on left are called lustres from the French and were intended to decorate the mantel. The two decanters on the right have white overlay on a cranberry color background.

They did not resemble that costlier glass but rather lace. Pieces from the 1830s, known by the generic name of lacy glass, have designs with American eagles and Yankee Clipper ships. Today they are prized Americana. It is simple to tell lacy glass from cut. Befitting its title, lacy is softer and does not scrape like cut glass.

Once perfected, this pressed method revolutionized the business. By 1836 other countries including England, Germany, and France used the same methods. By the 1850s three-fourths of American glass was pressed.

Art Glass

In the 1800s, as factories cranked out more and more glass, some artisans returned to ancient ways. Art Glass is blown glass and was part of that famous rebellion against machinery, the Arts and Crafts Movement. Tiffany or Galle, stars of Art Nouveau, would not have approved of factory-made glass but would have preferred art glass.

Depression Glass

The number one semi-antique is Depression Glass. This generic term defines mass-produced, inexpensive molded glass made from the late 1920s to the World War II era. It came in all the happy Art Deco colors: green, pink, blue, red, amber, and white. Many firms including Federal, Jeanette, and Hocking made it. How it got its name is a slice of "American pie" history.

As the depression in the 1930s hurt business, Americans searched for gimmicks to increase sales. Something like 1950s trading stamps or today's discount coupons was the result. When our relatives bought gas or went to a movie, a glass bowl or other pieces were given as a bonus. Seeing a film with Garbo or Barbara Stanwyck along with getting a free glass bowl may have boosted sales and morales.

Today that horrendous depression is mostly forgotten, but out of those dark times came this happy, colorful glass. Depression Glass is now an affordable and colorful semi-antique. Its popularity is justified.

Other molded glass from the 1920s and 1930s is easy to confuse with Depression Glass. This is also mass-produced glassware from the same decades. Refer to unsigned pieces as Depression Glass and the others by their signed names. Some famous ones are Heisey and Cambridge, both located in Ohio.

Recall our boycott of buying hometown antiques? That is certainly true about Heisey and Cambridge. Forget looking in Ohio. The Heisey company made first-rate pieces from 1896 to 1957. Most Heisey was marked with an "H" inside a diamond. However, sometimes paper labels were used. Heisey has a real quality feel, and its bottoms usually have a fluted design radiating from its center.

Cambridge, another terrific glass, was created in its name-sake city between 1901 and 1954. A "C" inside a triangle is its logo. Fostoria started in 1887 in Fostoria, Ohio and later moved to Moundsville, West Virginia, where it is still churning out quality yet reasonably priced glassware. It is usually marked "Fostoria."

How glass is decorated is another way of naming it. The ways are: cutting, etching, engraving, painting, or stenciling.

Cut Glass

Cut glass is easy to spot. Take the sensual approach and rub your palms over a bowl or compote. It is well-named because it literally cuts like sandpaper. Imitation cut glass feels duller, lacking this sharpness.

Antique cut glass is usually heavy and has thick walls. Objects are shaped by blowing with the mouth. Then the designs are literally cut into the glass with a metal or stone cutting wheel. In 1676 an Englishman, George Ravenscroft, added lead to the molten glass rendering it resilient and easy to cut.

The English, the Scots, and the Irish became known for first-rate cut glass and still are. The Irish are known for Waterford, the Scots for Stuart, and the English for Tudor. Since cut glass resembles rock crystal, it sometimes gets called crystal. Here is an appealing misnomer like that china one. Crystal is a quartz mineral. It gets confusing because transparent quartz resembles glass.

Americans made quality cut glass between 1880 and 1915. Those years mark the Golden Age of American cut glass and are charmingly called the Brilliant Period. Most is not signed and spotting a "John Hancock" is not easy. On a fruit bowl it is on the bottom part. To spot one take a piece outside on a sunny day. Move it around to find a signature. Magnifying glasses can help. Names are tough to spot, but once you find the first, others will

Photograph courtesy of Skinner, Inc.

The Victorians had a special serving piece whether in china, silver or glass for each part of the meal. This cut glass ice cream set from the late 1800s is in the "Russian" pattern.

Photograph courtesy of Skinner, Inc.

This 1900 cut glass piece with a silver rim was intended to hold tobacco.

be easier. Do not be too disappointed if yours lacks a signature. Eighty percent of cut glass was not signed. Some famous names are Libbey, Clark, Hawkes, Tuthil, Sterling Cut Glass, and one that will make you chuckle, Hoare.

An easy way to distinguish between modern and old cut glass involves that sensual approach. Our hands tell us that

Photograph courtesy of Skinner, Inc.

During Victorian times glass with sterling silver overlay was very popular such as these pieces from the late 1800s and early 1900s.

Photograph courtesy of Skinner, Inc.

Here is top-of-the-line hand blown and engraved Steuben Crystal by its famous designer Sidney Waugh. The engraved design of leaping gazelles seen on most of these pieces was a popular motif during the 1920s and 1930s.

modern is softer because it has been dipped in acid to remove sharp edges. Antique cut glass, so stylish these days, is expensive. A small chip can really reduce the price. Cracks and other problems blend so well with the cut decoration that they are hard to spot. We Group II collectors welcome those defects. A bouquet of roses can enjoy the same successful hiding effect as cracked plates displayed near the ceiling.

Engraved and etched glass are miniversions of cut glass because the decorating processes are somewhat similar.

Engraved Glass

Engraved patterns are produced by applying emery powder mixed with oil to the edges of small revolving copper discs. Engraving with a diamond, known for cutting glass, was used before the wheel. Stemware monogramming uses this method because the designs are shallower than cut glass.

Etched Glass

Hydrofluoric acid etches designs into glass. The parts to remain plain are coated with wax. The design is scratched upon the nonwaxed area where the hydrochloric acid actually carves the design into the glass.

Antique glass is one of the best deals going. It is beautiful, old, and reasonably priced. If you are considering something to collect, it is a perfect choice. Imagine how elegant a champagne toast will be when sipped from antique stemware.

Read on to learn about one more needed ingredient to complete this antiques dining fantasy.

25

Silver

The word silver is derived from the Greek term argyos, meaning bright and shiny. Working with this metal goes as far back as making glass, furniture, or pottery. An always-in-demand antique, it continuously increases in value. Rest assured that we antiquers will be able to discover some stunning pieces at affordable prices.

Silver has two appealing purposes: they usually revolve around eating and drinking. They have two classifications. Holloware is for bowls, tankards, teapots, sugar bowls, and other pieces. Religious holloware crafted from this valuable natural resource includes chalices, beakers, wine glasses, and spice boxes. Flatware refers to knives, forks, spoons, and other utensils.

Silver, as found in nature, is pretty limp. It is strengthened by adding copper during its melted stage. Around 1300, during the reign of Edward I, English silversmiths organized the process of silversmithing. Those clever Brits, as with ceramics, are very tidy. They regulated the quantity of copper added to silver by creating the sterling standard. Sterling silver is a recipe which requires 925 cups/parts pure silver and 75 cups/parts of copper needed for durability. Although not pure silver, this concoction is as close as anyone born with a spoon you-know-where would want. A piece of pure silver cutlery would be so flimsy it would bend easily.

The origin of the word sterling is interesting. One theory is that it is derived from the name Easterling. Easterlings were

Photograph courtesy of Skinner, Inc.

This English silver and cut glass centerpiece or epergne was for the center of the dining table. This dates from the George IV era. The lions at its feet make it very Neoclassical/Regency looking.

German silversmiths who came to England in the Middle Ages. The second is from the word starling (little star), an early mark for English silver.

The British system of hallmarks really deserves our applause. These labels tell us the item's age and origin. On the back of a spoon there are usually some marks where the handle meets the bowl.

If a piece is English sterling, it will have a rectangular box with a design of a crouching lion. The *Lion Passant* mark first started in London about 1554. Looking for what I call the Leo the Lion mark is the first step to determine if your item is sterling.

Pieces usually have other hallmarks revealing more information. Think of them as a label inside a shirt stating content, maker, and laundry directions. Leo the Lion is the only one needed to be memorized. The others are easy to decode with a book on British hallmarks.

Hallmarks are usually jumbled without any order. After Leo, the next important one identifies the city of origin. These are tougher to learn, so keep a reference work handy. To decipher the remaining marks, you need to know the object's hometown. Each center has a symbol. The leopard's head, for London, seems to be a whimsical image for such a regal city. Others are represented by an anchor for Birmingham, a crown for Sheffield, a harp for Dublin, and so on.

After identifying its origin, the next hallmark is terrific because it tells the year the item was made. After you find the city, then look for a single letter. Match letters under the city of origin, and presto, you have the exact dates. This custom started about 1438. After 1784 it gets easier. The profile of the ruler became an extra hallmark. George III's tells us it is from his day. A young Victoria without her acquired Rococo figure, instantly pinpoints a piece from the early days of her reign.

The next hallmark is the maker's mark or monogram, and usually has two letters, such as H.B. Your silver book also gives the name. The B is for Bateman and the H for Hester, that noteworthy 1700s achiever.

Knowing furniture styles really helps to date silver. Its designs copied furniture. A 1730s pepper castor (shaker) has feet, called trifid, almost identical to the cabriole legs of Queen Anne furniture. A helmet-shaped teapot by the Bateman family repeats the shape of Hepplewhite shield-back chairs.

European silver is at the graduate school level of antiques. They did not mark things as neatly as those Brits. They also used 825 or 800 parts pure silver to 175 or 200 parts copper added for strength. Get intimate with British and Yankee silver first, and then you will be ready for continental pieces.

American silversmiths before the mid-1800s did not use the British standard for sterling. They followed the coin gauge. This used less pure silver than sterling. Nine hundred parts pure silver with 100 parts copper was the basic recipe for American coins and silver pieces. Most 900/1000 pieces, whether a spoon or a bowl, feel very light. They were not marked with a number or a lion. Rather the silvermaker's name was put into a small box. In the colonies, New England was a center of silvermaking. Hull and Sanderson around 1659 were very early silversmiths, and of course the most famous from the 1700s is Paul Revere.

Photograph courtesy of Skinner, Inc.

Here are some American coin silver porringers/bowls. The stein-looking piece is a cann. All date from the 1700s.

There are several good books to guide you in identifying American silvermakers. They all have much information about Paul Revere II (1735-1818). This gent was the son of a French Protestant who came to Boston for religious freedom. His real name was Rivoire which he Americanized. Mostly noted as a patriot, this artisan also crafted fine silver. He gave up his business for five years during the American Revolution. Undecorated Revere bowls and pitchers are synonymous with the Neoclassical style that he loved to craft.

Just before the Civil War, American silvermakers switched to the British standard of sterling silver. They marked 925/1000 on items to make it easier to identify. Newer American items use the word sterling, usually indicating post 1860 production.

Photographs courtesy of Skinner, Inc.

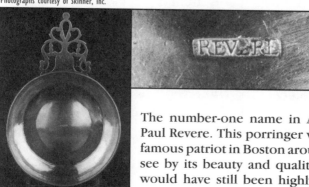

The number-one name in American silver is Paul Revere. This porringer was created by the famous patriot in Boston around 1754. You can see by its beauty and quality that Mr. Revere would have still been highly collectible even without that Longfellow poem.

Photograph courtesy of Skinner, Inc.

Examples of that French word "*Repoussé*," meaning pushed out in English. Use French in this instance as the Yankee word does not do justice to these mid to late 1800s examples of *Repoussé* by Kirk, Jacobi, and Jenkins of Baltimore.

In making silver holloware in England or America, the metal was rolled or hammered into thin sheets. These were beaten into the shape of a teapot or bowl. Then the surface was decorated. One manner was chasing, which is like engraving. Piercing was a technique that cut holes into the side of a bowl making it appear like a basket.

Repoussé, the most beautiful decorating technique for silver, is justifiably called by its French name. My apologies for not using the English equivalent, but the French win this one. The term sounds more polished in their tongue than in ours. "Pushed out" does not even come close to capturing the radiance of *Repoussé* pieces. The almost three-dimensional decoration is hammered from the underside of a silver piece; hence, it is literally pushed out. Mr. Revere remains the most famous silversmith, but another celebrated American silversmith made *Repoussé* the most renowned pattern.

Samuel Kirk (1793-1872) of Baltimore wisely gave the name *Repoussé* to his flatware and holloware decorated in this fashion. Certainly Kirk's *Repoussé* is the all-time-most-cherished flatware in this country. This antique pattern gets higher prices at auctions than other designs.

Sterling silver or coin silver pieces are lighter in feeling than silverplate. Sterling silver is still somewhat wimpy when compared to comparable silverplated pieces. Silver spoons can be easily bent. A plated one is more rigid due to the stronger metal under its silver coating.

Silver pieces were expensive, and finally some silversmith came up with the process of making less costly silverplated items. By the mid-1700s the British came up with a successful way of making items appear totally crafted from silver when they were not. Thomas Boulsover of Sheffield, England was a pioneer in this field. Sheffield is to English silverplate what Staffordshire is to English china.

The generic term Sheffield is a 1700s silverplating technique done in that city. The procedure was like making a sandwich. Two outside silver sheets are the bread while copper in the center is the cheese. Two silver sheets were pounded thin, and a thicker piece of copper was placed between them. The

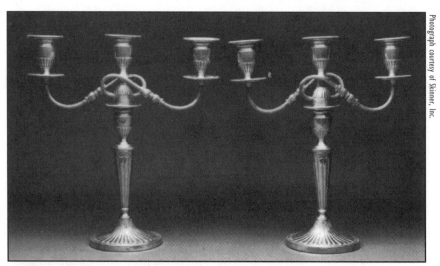

Photograph courtesy of Skinner, Inc.

These very Neoclassical 1800 Shefield plated three-light candelabra originally may have adorned a Hepplewhite or Sheraton sideboard.

sandwich showing only silver was shaped into teapots, trays, or whatever. All hand done and less expensive than sterling, Sheffield plate still remained out of reach for most.

Before 1784 most Sheffield plate was unmarked. The weight of an item is a good clue to determine if it is plate. A Sheffield plated tray is heavier and more rigid than sterling. Worn spots reveal the copper just as missing veneer shows the less expensive wood under the costlier one. This is the patina or the antique look of Sheffield that makes it so special.

Around 1840 the Industrial Revolution also changed the silverplating business. As machines began making less costly items for homes such as furniture and glass pieces, manufacturers did the same for silverplated pieces. The Elkington Brothers in Birmingham, England applied for a patent around 1840 for a new way to make silverplate.

This novel system that transformed the silver business is called electroplating. It involved the immersion of a teapot to be coated with another metal by electrolytic action. The base or underneath metal of the teapot was silver-looking. It was dipped in a bath containing an electrolytic solution. When an electric current was passed through the water, particles of silver transferred evenly to the outside of the teapot. How much silver was applied depended on how many plunges. Also, the items to be plated could be molded which was quicker than the handshaping needed for Sheffield.

Photograph courtesy of Skinner, Inc.

This electroplated hot water urn was placed next to the tea pot and kept hot water at hand when more tea was needed. This English one was made during the early years of the rule of Queen Victoria.

Photograph courtesy of Skinner, Inc.

This American silver plated Reed and Barton ice water pitcher dates from the 1880s and in furniture terms it is in the Renaissance Revival style. In the days before modern refrigerators, it kept cold water on the sideboard in the dining room.

Electroplating changed everything related to silver. It ended costlier Sheffield plating and practically wiped out the pewter business.

In 1847 the Roger Brothers in America started making silverplate. They used the same high-tech process as the Elkington firm. Rumors still persist that the they swiped the secret from those British boys.

Anything silverplate, whether English or American, will not have the Lion Rampant mark, the word Sterling, or 925/1000. The word Sheffield found on a piece of plated holloware indicates youth. British pieces were marked with E.P.N.S. meaning electroplate on nickel silver. American pieces usually had the companies' name such as Gorham or Reed and Barton. Sometimes "triple dipped" or three *** would be seen. They meant items were dipped three times into the electric solution for a triple coat of silver.

This is worth repeating: silverplate is usually heavier than a comparable sterling item. The sterling version, such as a tea-spoon, can be easily bent while a plated one is inflexible. That same information rule about ceramics is certainly true with silver. The more details on a label such as length of a tray or its pattern's name, the newer it is.

Here is a fun story about an antique silver item. Monteith bowls about nine inches in diameter and four inches high were

This is an early 1900s English Monteith bowl named after that famous Scotsman, Mr. Monteith, who rumor has it was the first to add booze to the fruit punch.

Photograph courtesy of Skinner, Inc.

a favorite wedding present to give in the early 1900s. This silver punch bowl has a notched top where pedestal-based glasses can be attached. Its picturesque rumor of origin, like other antiques fables, has not been authenticated. This antique was named after a Mr. Monteith, a Scottish party boy, who legend says invented the habit of adding booze to punch.

As the Victorian upper and middle classes grew, so did their craving for silver. Whether using sterling or humbler plate, they had everything imaginable in that metal. Things got as complicated as today's myriad sports shoes. Once, there were only

Photograph courtesy of Skinner, Inc.

Meriden made this silver plated coffee and tea service in the 1880s. It matches the grandeur of a Renaissance Revival sideboard.

gym shoes. Different models are now required for jogging, weight lifting, handball, and other sports. The same was true when it came to the Victorian flatware. There were many different spoons for dining. Genteel etiquette demanded a small one for after dinner coffee, a pointed one for melons, a tiny model for salt cellars, and even a half spoon and half fork, called an ice cream fork, for cake and ice cream.

Old Sheffield plate holloware and flatware are very expensive, but when it comes to electroplate, there are plenty of bargains. Plate does not have the resale value as sterling. That means there are some deals for us. A silverplate tea service can cost seventy-five percent less than a comparable sterling one. Just think of plate as veneered with silver. Sterling and plate tarnish at the same rate, and no one but you will be able to the tell the difference.

Let's go on to get acquainted with an antiques cousin of silver.

26

Pewter

In the late 1700s, pewter was the non-rich person's substitute for costlier silver pieces. Today pewter, like many antiques of humble origins, has become very upscale.

Pewter is an alloy of metals resembling silver. Tin is the main ingredient with small additions of lead, copper, antimony, and bismuth.

It is easy to distinguish pewter from silver because it is duller looking and heavier than its aristocratic cousin. Remember the heftier, the better the quality.

Pewter has existed since the days of the Egyptians and Romans. First made in England in the 1100s, it was usually for religious purposes such as chalices. By the 1600s, pewter was used by the small-but-beginning-to-grow middle class.

Pewter from the early 1700s to about 1840 was widely used in England and the United States. It was the Tupperware of its time. The better-off masses used it for everything from spoons, to beer tankards, to measuring cups. Royal families would never have supped from pewter. Their dining services customarily included gold or silver plates or tankards, and those silver spoons that came with their births.

By the late 1700s, pewter production adapted to the advances made possible by machinery. It could be cast, shaped around a mold, spun, and easily cut to form many useful objects. Spinning involves a thin plate of pewter rotating rapidly on a lathe which forces it to take the shape of the wooden core. The

Photograph courtesy of Skinner, Inc.

This pewter coffee pot was probably made in Philadelphia around the time of the Revolution. It is pure Neoclassical style from its very Roman looking urn finial to its elongated urn shaped body and square pedestal base.

metal was cast in flat pieces. Then it was rolled into sheets to the desired thickness and hammered into shape. Holloware was cast in molds, usually in sections, and then soldered together. The seam marks were then smoothed with hand tools.

Ceramic and silverplated household items created pewter's downfall. Mr. Wedgwood, Mr. Spode, and other potters perfected the mass production of pewter's main rival. By the early 1800s, inexpensive and quality china was readily available. Ceramics did not tarnish like pewter and were easier to clean. If that was not enough, dishes came decorated. How could staid pewter compete with crockery that came in blue and white, and other colors?

There was even more competition. In the 1840s, silver electroplating was perfected. This modern way of coating silver over a less expensive metal gave the look of sterling silver for less outlay. Always up on the latest, the Victorians preferred silverplate and ceramics to b-l-a-h pewter. Most pewter production ended. How ironic because this antique, one of the first to benefit from the technology of the Industrial Revolution, became its early victim.

Thomas Bumstead of Boston was a pioneer pewterer who started in 1654. Between 1700 and 1850 America had 200 pewterers. Everything from tankards, porringers, and plates filled American homes.

Photograph courtesy of Skinner, Inc.

Popular utilitarian pieces in European, American, and English pewter from the late 1700s and early 1800s are plates, candlesticks, and measures. The large round piece in the back is called a charger.

Some claim that American pewter was not as good as English. The Brits had to mark theirs, so there is the tendency to regard unmarked pewter as American. That can be misleading. Some Yankee pewter was labeled, and also global trade has been going on for centuries. New unmarked English found its way into many American homes.

A famous 1790s American touch mark is the eagle. This popular motif was thought to be the symbol of our early federal government. Eagles are also decorations on tops of gilt Sheraton-style mirrors from the early 1800s. State seals of Massachusetts and Rhode Island were often used. From the 1780s until the 1860s, the United States was a major supplier. The important names in American pewter are Danforth, Boardman, Melville, Sellew, Flagg, and Homan.

A subgroup of pewter, invented in the mid-1700s, is Britannia. This metallic alloy lacks lead. It replaced pewter that contained lead which they considered unhealthy. This new "pewter" used by the Brits and Yanks adapted very easily to machine production. It was often called white metal because it looks more like silver than the older model.

The same fate happened to American pewter as to its British cousin. As the demand for pewter fizzled, some makers such as

Flagg and Homan wisely switched to the more lucrative silverplating business. As the Industrial Revolution grew, Britannia, like pewter, fell from favor.

During the 1920s as antiques became chic, American manufacturers (as with furniture) started reproducing antique pewter. These flapper versions are now semi-antiques. They offer value because they are well-made and affordable. When "pewter," or something similar appears on its bottom, the piece is a twentieth-century reproduction. Like most items, the more information, the newer it is. Stieff Pewter Company always labeled their wonderful pieces this way: "Authentic Williamsburg Reproduction."

Should tarnished pewter be polished? There are arguments for and against. When new, it was shiny, so that is the "pro." The "con" says that dullness makes it look antique, a valued trait to be protected. The choice is yours. Just avoid scratching the pewter when polishing.

Pewter by famous makers usually commands big bucks. Why not collect pieces in the same leagues as those anonymous paintings? Buy unsigned pieces. If you find a plate or platter with a bent rim, clear a spot on your highest book shelf.

Like pine, that other relic with an unpretentious ancestry, pewter was once the wallflower of antiques. Today that silliness is gone, and pewter finally flourishes as a top-notch antique.

27

Art Nouveau I: Tea, Champagne, and Waltzes at the Ritz

In 1898 during the last decade of the reign of Queen Victoria, the Frenchman Cesar Ritz (1850-1918) opened in Paris the most luxurious inn the world had ever seen, the Hotel Ritz. Soon its name became synonymous with opulence. It was so successful Mr. Ritz in 1905 opened his second hotel in London. "Tea at the Ritz" for Londoners became a fashionable pastime. The Parisians probably had a similar habit but involving, of course, champagne. By 1929 Irving Berlin wrote a song, "Putting on the Ritz," which became a 1930 Hollywood movie. During these years when many of the blue stocking set partook of tea and champagne and waltzed at the two Hotels Ritz, another style emerged.

The adjective, ritzy, coined from the name of the Ritz Hotels certainly conveys the lavishness of Art Nouveau in its first stage. This fashion followed the Arts and Crafts "handmade" philosophy. Just as a stay or sipping tea at the Ritz was not affordable for everyone, the same was true for most early Art Nouveau objects.

Meaning "modern art" in French, it started in France where machinery was never appreciated as much as in Britain or in America. By 1890 the style arrived in the United States and lasted until World War I. Art Nouveau followed Rococo Revival's ornateness. These two shared traits such as cabriole legs, shell motifs, and floral carvings. Art Nouveau used those motifs with a slightly different kink, carrying the curvy feeling of the earlier design further. The most striking trademark about

Photograph courtesy of Skinner, Inc.

This poster by Paul Berthon from 1900 personifies the Art Nouveau style. The lady depicted has long flowing hair and the flowers droop like a bouquet of tulips just before the petals fall.

Art Nouveau, whether a spoon or a stained-glass window, is the flowing look of its designs.

Its visual impact is easy to fathom. Imagine a Rococo Revival sofa that is made from plastic. As the sun shines, it starts to melt. The roses, cabriole legs, and the general shape of the settee are beginning to run like lava oozing from a volcano. This is the flowing look, Art Nouveau's number one design emblem. This style has no sharp edges. It is not low-keyed and is even more highly strung and more flamboyant than Rococo Revival.

Loomism: It is easy to remember that flow rhymes with nouveau. This keeps us from getting this style confused with a later design, Art Deco.

Art Nouveau's curvy style was seen in all aspects of home furnishings. Its designs are from a 1900 garden full of delicate

This Art Nouveau lady captured in 1896 by Louis Rhead almost looks Medieval (following Arts and Crafts beliefs). The lily blossom is another favorite flower.

Photograph courtesy of Skinner, Inc.

lilies, roses, morning glories, or tulips waiting to be transformed into stained glass, silver pieces, furniture, lamp shades, ornate subway entrances, and even a department store.

Most of Art Nouveau's ornate designs, whether silver, furniture, or glass, had to be handmade. Factory production was not yet able to duplicate its opulence. That pleased French artisans. Along with fellow Arts and Crafts followers in Britain and America, they were like the back-to-mother-nature enthusiasts of the 1960s who worked mostly by hand.

The Universal Exposition of 1889 transformed Paris in two beautiful ways. The Eiffel Tower, the fair's symbol, was controversial because it was so tall and its "bare-bones" construction showing its framework was considered too stark for that artistic city of churches and museums. At 984 feet, it was the highest man-made structure in the world, a forerunner to the modern skyscraper. Today Paris would not be Paris without that famous landmark. The second way the city would be forever modified was by the handcrafted objects displayed in its exhibitions.

Photograph courtesy of Skinner, Inc.

This 1848 view of a cathedral by Belgian artist Jules Victor Genison (1805-1860) shows Gothic arches and those stained-glass windows that so influenced the art of Louis Comfort Tiffany.

They would eventually be seen in many French artifacts and buildings dating from this era that today is called Art Nouveau.

Then in 1895, following Art Nouveau's success at the 1889 Fair, the German art dealer Samuel Bing (1838-1905) opened in Paris a boutique called "the Art Nouveau House." Art Nouveau glass, jewelry, posters, and other delights were offered with ritzy price tags.

Bing's boutique did so well that at the next Paris Fair, the 1900 one, he displayed even more Art Nouveau beauties. There were chairs and even glass shades to cover the nakedness of the recently invented electric light bulb. Today in the D'Orsay Museum, not far from the site of the fair, some of these superb antiques are displayed.

When mentioning Art Nouveau and the light bulb, one person comes to mind immediately. American Louis Comfort Tiffany (1848-1933) is to Art Nouveau as Chippendale is to English 1700s furniture. His father Charles L. (d. 1902) founded in 1834 in New York City the fine jewelry establishment, Tiffany and Company. Young Tiffany analyzed early Christian mosaics in Ravenna, Italy. These religious pictures were created from small pieces of stone, marble, or glass held together in mortar. He also studied in France the stained-glass windows located at the Gothic cathedral of Chartres.

In the 1800s, stained-glass windows were usually crafted by painting ground-up powdered colored glass to the surface of clear. Tiffany came up with his novel method adapted from the Italian mosaics. He pieced a segment of green glass to suggest a leaf, a red one for a blossom, and so on. All were held together by lead to create a mosaic picture. If human parts were needed, Mr. Tiffany used the old way of painting on the glass to suggest a hand or face. His 1900 masterpiece, "The Four Seasons," depicts the changes of the year as shown through various floral designs.

The magical effect of the sun's rays shining through his stained glass thrilled Mr. Tiffany. Therefore, he located his glass in places like stair landings to best capture this gift from nature.

A true Arts and Crafts person, Mr. Tiffany hated the pollution caused by the Industrial Revolution. His art softened the view of the damaged outside. By being able to observe it through one of his creations, the impression of the outside improved. Those windows made everything look nicer. Too bad Mr. Tifffany cannot be given credit for that cliche "looking at the world through rose-colored glass" because that is exactly what he did for us.

Photograph courtesy of Skinner, Inc.

This 1908 etching by Joseph Pennell (American 1857-1926) appropriately entitled "On the Way to Bessemer," is exactly the type of view that Mr. Tiffany tried to improve by viewing the world through his stained-glass windows.

Photograph courtesy of Skinner, Inc.

A picture is worth one thousand...so no further words. A Tiffany window from 1904, entitled "Portrait Pictorial Window."

Tiffany's windows brought him enormous success, and his name became synonymous with stained-glass windows. Tiffany has become a generic term along with that other fellow Arts and Crafts believer, Mr. Morris as in Morris chairs!

People say they have a Tiffany window when they really mean one that may have been crafted by his studio or by one of his contemporary competitors. His are usually signed. His dream home, Laurelton Hall, on Long Island in New York, housed breathtaking furniture, windows, and light fixtures with stained-glass shades.

A Tiffany lamp usually has a dark green bronze base resembling a branch of a tree with a mushroom-shaped shade. The stained-glass top usually portrayed flowers such

An unsigned leaded-glass scenic landscape window costs less than a signed Tiffany one. It captures Art Nouveau with designs of tree, flowers, and background hills.

Photograph courtesy of Skinner, Inc.

as chrysanthemums, poppies, or peonies. The glow coming from a deep red poppy shade has a magical effect as it makes the light less harsh. Electricity, then a high-tech wonder, was beautified and coordinated with the room's furnishings by Mr. Tiffany's art. So Mr. Art Nouveau ended up improving the inside panorama, too. This is an example of the union of art and science that started in Art Nouveau and really grew in the Art Deco style of the 1920s and 1930s.

A genuine Tiffany bronze base should read "Tiffany Studios" or "Tiffany Furnaces" and usually has a number on its base. Glass lamp shades should be marked either "LCT" for Louis Comfort Tiffany or "Favrile," the name of his glass line. The shades were usually numbered. Tiffany lamps have sold at

A Tiffany bronze inkwell depicts a crab in a circular motif that captures the feeling of waves washing upon the beach.

Photograph courtesy of Skinner, Inc.

auction for well over $100,000! When new it may have cost about $110. That was much dough for those days. Remember that was when a nickel at the local pub bought a beer that included a free lunch. Those certainly were the good old days— a brew, a lunch, and a real Tiffany lamp, all for $100.05.

Photograph courtesy of Skinner, Inc.

A pair of Tiffany four-light "Lily" lamps really define the Art Nouveau style.

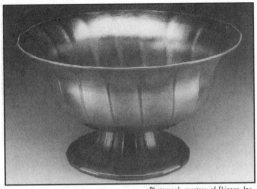

A 1902 iridescent gold-colored punch bowl made by the Quezel firm, a group of ex-Tiffany employees. This is another example of how every great artist from Tiffany to Chippendale to Wedgwood were often copied.

Photograph courtesy of Skinner, Inc.

Tiffany never stopped crafting Art Nouveau wonders. His Favrile glass, all handblown, had a secret recipe of special chemicals to create its iridescent quality. These were added when the sand was molten. His incandescent vases are so flowing and lightweight looking that they resemble lilies just picked from the garden.

Favrile glass brings up an interesting point about antiques. It is natural to assume the older an antique, the more valuable. However, age is no guarantee. Tiffany's vases dating around 1900 can yield $3,000 or even more at auction. A Roman glass vase about 1,900 years older can sell at auction for a tenth of the younger Tiffany one.

L.C.T. certainly practiced what he created right down to his granted death wish. At 85, in true Art Nouveau form, he was buried under 300 pink carnations.

The other Art Nouveau superstar is, of course, Emile Galle (1846-1904), the French Tiffany. Naturally, the French would insist that Tiffany is the American Galle. Either way we antiquers are grateful to both of them.

Galle used flowing Art Nouveau designs such as raspberries on his glass vases. A vase was first shaped in flexible wax, then a metal mold was made from the wax model. Then molten glass was poured into the form to produce Art Nouveau shapes. His antiques are a beautiful reminder of those times of tea, champagne, and waltzes at the Ritz.

Like glass, silver adapts easily to Art Nouveau's fluid demands whether a teapot or a teaspoon. Art Nouveau silver

Photograph courtesy of Skinner, Inc.

This German Brass and Copper punch set circa 1905 manages to capture Art Nouveau's excessive curviness, especially in the bowl's legs.

flatware is usually decorated with floral motifs such as morning glories entwining the handle of a teaspoon. By 1900, American silver firms began making Art Nouveau styled flatware. These patterns include Wallace's "Peony" (1906), Reed and Barton's "Les Cinq Fleurs" (the Five Flowers) (1900), and Gorham's "Imperial Chrysanthemum" (1894). Their names in true Art Nouveau spirit revolve around flowers.

The 1889 and 1900 Paris World's Fairs, which established Art Nouveau, also boost the status of two American potteries. Both Grueby and Rookwood won gold medals at those two exhibitions. Another famous one was Newcomb College Pottery. These Arts and Crafts potteries really used clay's natural shapeability to achieve ceramic wonders capturing Art Nouveau's flow.

Grueby, Newcomb, and Rookwood, unlike the two English china makers, Wedgwood or

Photograph curtesy of Cincinnati Art Galleries.

This 1909 Rookwood vase really captures the sweeping feeling of Art Nouveau.

This oak chair made in Finland circa 1905 explains visually how hard it was to turn rigid wood into Art Nouveau. The cutout and pierced panels below the armrest help give a lighter look, but the chair still remains very inflexible looking.

Photograph courtesy of Skinner, Inc.

Copeland Spode, were more artistically than business inclined. The establishments were "art potteries" meaning profit was not as important as creativity. Rookwood, founded in 1880 by Maria Longworth Nichols in Cincinnati, Ohio, was known for its innovatively designed Art Nouveau pieces. It sadly closed in 1960. Mrs. Nichols would be thrilled to learn that a few years ago a vase by one of her artists sold at auction for over $180,000.

In 1895 Newcomb College Pottery was established in New Orleans, Louisianna. Like the other two ceramicists, Newcomb used many Art Nouveau designs such as wisteria, magnolias, and palm trees. Most pieces before 1920 were one-of-a-kind. The Depression caused Newcomb to close in 1930.

Bostonian William H. Grueby (1867-1925) began Grueby Pottery in 1894. The individually decorated pieces are the most collected. Even Tiffany obtained Grueby pottery to use as lamp bases for his shades. That is quite an endorsement! A vase by Ruth Erikson that around 1899 cost about $50 will sell today for thousands. Grueby went bankrupt in 1908, a fate that seemed unavoidable to most art potteries.

Art Nouveau's flowing designs worked well in silver, ceramics, and glass. Turning wood into an elongated Art Nouveau chair was no easy task. Besides his work in glass, Emile Galle succeeded at making chairs, tables, and beds capturing Art

Photograph courtesy of Skinner, Inc.

A mahogany table with floral marquetry top by Emile Galle. Its inlay and curvy legs give the table an Art Nouveau feeling.

Nouveau's cascading designs. It is hard to fathom that these pieces were crafted from a rigid tree.

Louis Majorelle (1859-1926), a French contemporary of Galle, was another Art Nouveau star. The headboards of Majorelle's beds look like flower petals. His chairs of lily blossom designs were very costly. Galle's and Majorelle's accomplishments are displayed at the Musee d'Orsay.

The factory renditions of most Victorian-era styles such as Eastlake, Renaissance Revival, and Rococo Revival furniture were geared for the middle class. Ornate Art Nouveau furniture, on the other hand, was almost impossible to adapt to machine production. So it remained mostly handcrafted and not a big hit for the middle class because few could afford it.

Art Nouveau antiques from its first period are still too ritzy for most antiquers. The first stage dating from the 1890s is Art Nouveau I, the era of tea, champagne, and waltzes at the Ritz. Objects were crafted by hand, and today most are in museums or belong to the rich and famous. Get intimate with Tiffany lamps and Galle art glass by visiting them at museums.

By the early 1900s some items in the manner of the trendsetters such as Mr. Tiffany were being made in mass quantities. There are some Art Nouveau treasures waiting for us, but first we are going to meet the most luscious Art Nouveau building in the world!

Art Nouveau II: Meet You at Carson's

We are about to visit one of the greatest Art Nouveau accomplishments in the world. We can even touch it because it has no museum ropes. No admission fee is charged; in fact, entry is greatly solicited. You will not find it in Paris or New York, but in downtown Chicago, Illinois.

Paris and London may have their Ritz Hotels, but Chicago has Carson, Pirie, Scott department store designed by Louis Henry Sullivan (1856-1924). Mr. Sullivan is the Tiffany of American architecture. Representing Yankee ingenuity, the Midwestern architect blended the French Art Nouveau to the American invention, the skyscraper. The results are still sensational. Erected approximately at the same time as the Paris Ritz, between 1899-1904, Carson's is a twelve-storied building decorated with flowing Art Nouveau floral motifs. Sullivan designed a very high-tech building whose skeletal support system dictated the outward appearance of the structure. Walls no longer had to be thick because the hidden beams supplied the support. This allowed lots of windows similar to 1950s picture windows to let in much light and air.

In 1900 eyes, the store seemed ultra modern, perhaps almost sterile when compared to other Chicago landmarks such as the Auditorium Hotel. Most buildings then were as ornate as a Renaissance Revival sideboard.

His technique for flowing up the staid facade parades his genius. As a sand castle at the beach can be decorated by

Below: An early photograph of the Art Nouveau Carson, Pirie, Scott department store in Chicago as designed by Louis Henry Sullivan. Right: This view shows large windows called Chicago windows or picture window. Notice how the plainer upper stories reveal the steel skeletal support system.

Photographs courtesy of Carson Pirie Scott.

Photographs courtesy of Carson Pirie Scott.

Left: The cast iron ornamentation looks almost Parisian, but it is Chicago-created Art Nouveau. Top: A close view of the Art Nouveau ornamentation.

dribbling sand, Sullivan did a similar ploy to glamorize his building. To make his masterpiece less stark, he applied iron ornamentation in sweeping Art Nouveau floral designs to soften the straight look of the building.

Carson, Pirie, Scott, and Company building represents the second level of Art Nouveau. It is the triumphal meeting of the two stages of Art Nouveau. Its ornate Art Nouveau facade follows Galle's and Tiffany's designs, but it did something more wonderful than their art ever accomplished. Sullivan's superb work brought Art Nouveau's beauty to the masses as they shopped at the State Street emporium.

Leave those ritzy Art Nouveau antiques for museums and the tea and champagne crowd at the Ritz. Find out what we Group II Collectors get in the antique Art Nouveau department.

Around 1905, some Art Nouveau designs were mass produced and sold in stores like Carson's. These items were more affordable than the individually crafted versions. Today they are tempting antiques with nonstressful prices. In the early 1900s, Art Nouveau entered in its Second Stage, the mass production one, much to the horror of the Arts and Crafts followers.

Photograph courtesy of Skinner, Inc.

A parlor suite by Karpen Brothers made for middle of the road consumers. Notice the cabriole legs. The splats are very Art Nouveau with the flowing floral motif and carved cherub type head in the back crest.

Right: Handel's less-affluent-person's version of a Tiffany lamp from the early 1900s. Its base was gilded metal to resemble costlier bronze used on the Tiffany models.

Photograph courtesy of Skinner, Inc.

Photograph courtesy of Skinner, Inc.

Left: This mass-produced English armchair from 1905 manages very successfully to capture the sweeping look of Art Nouveau due to its construction from thin pieces of wood. The insert shows the flower and vine detailing on the crest rail.

A very popular Art Nouveau item among middle Americans was Royal Dux porcelain. It was made in Czechoslovakia in the early 1900s such as these two vases with fully dimensional figures.

Photograph courtesy of Skinner, Inc.

Here is an Art Nouveau antique within reach for most: Carnival glass. This molded glass with a colorful iridescent finish and Art Nouveau droopiness was made in huge quantities. Its joyful name was accidentally earned. Factories around 1905 tried unsuccessfully to duplicate the colors of Tiffany's Favrile line. They ended up with an orange glass that some considered so garish it must have come from a carnival. That happy name has stuck prompting thoughts of Ferris Wheels and cotton candy. Whether in the shape of a fruit bowl or vase renditions, it graced many sideboards between 1905 and the 1920s, and now is considered antique.

Photograph courtesy of Skinner, Inc.

This very Parisian looking lady is promoting American Schrafft's Ice Cream on this early 1900s poster. Advertizing posters successfully brought Art Nouveau designs to middle Americans.

Photograph courtesy of Cincinnati Art Galleries.

Weller Pottery brought the beauty of Art Nouveau to the masses in the early twentieth century. Today Weller is a highly-collected antique.

Photograph courtesy of Cincinnati Art Galleries.

Roseville also brought Art Nouveau designs first created on Rookwood, Grueby, and Newcomb Potteries to the masses.

There are plenty of vases and compotes by Dugan Glass, Imperial Glass, Millersburg Glass, and McKee Glass in the $100 price range at malls everywhere. Buy carnival glass from reputable retailers because hard-to-detect reproductions have been made since the 1950s.

Sterling dresser sets with floral Art Nouveau designs could easily be made by machines. They adorned many 1910 dressing tables. Reed and Barton, Wallace, and other silver factories produced sets consisting of hand mirror, hair brush, nail files, covered jars, hair receivers, and clothes brushes. Motifs were usually floral such as poppies or lilies. Buy unmatching yet similarly designed pieces, and you can get a "married" set quite reasonably.

Buying sterling silver teaspoons can really add up quickly. If you were not born with any you know where, choose silver plated Art Nouveau flatware. Unfortunately, old silverplate doesn't hold up in value which is good news when we want to buy some. Silverplated flatware is just as good looking as the sterling version. Shelling out $5 for a teaspoon in the Art Nouveau pattern "Vintage," made by Rogers, rather than $45 for a silver one in "Peony" makes plate all the sweeter. It is not any less beautiful, and besides it tarnishes at the same rate!

While those big three art potteries, Grueby, Newcomb, and Rookwood crafted ritzy ceramics, others geared their products to Main Street homes. They borrowed ideas from those upscale ones.

Zanesville, Ohio, became a pottery center in the early 1900s. Its nickname "Clay City" was due to its large deposits of that natural resource needed for ceramics.

Roseville and Weller, two Zanesville potteries, mass produced Art Nouveau ceramics copying Grueby, Newcomb, and Rookwood. These less costly ones offer similar designs and have graduated from garage sales to antiques stores. They deserve that status, but elevated position brings increased prices. They are still more affordable than pottery from earlier ones.

Samuel A. Weller (1851-1925) introduced the "Louwelsea" line resembling Rookwood in the 1890s. Weller brought Art

Nouveau's beauty to many homes but finally ceased in 1949. Another "Clay City" pottery, Roseville, was very successful and created many vases in the 1930s and 1940s that can be found in shops today for under $100. Sadly, in 1954 Roseville closed. We can easily spot Weller vases with an incised mark on bottom and Roseville with its label: "Rozanne, R.P.CO."

In the mid 1800s, as machines made less expensive yet quality European china, a new pastime started. Factories such as the Hutschenreuther in Germany, Arnfeldt in France,

Photograph courtesy of Skinner, Inc.

A 1905 English oak sideboard, although quite massive, captures the Art Nouveau feeling by its incised carved panels on the door fronts and the leaded window in the top central piece.

Photograph courtesy of Skinner, Inc.

Mass-produced and quality oak pieces followed the plainness of the Stickly originals. They were very popular with many Americans. This china cabinet from 1910 often gets called "Golden Oak" because as the finish ages it mellowed into that hue.

and Lenox in America produced undecorated ceramics called "porcelain blank." A plate left the factory undecorated, or "blank." An amateur artist would paint it at home. China decorating is how Maria Longworth Nichols got interested in pottery which ultimately led to Rookwood Pottery.

By 1900, china painting was quite popular and followed many Art Nouveau designs. A saucer or plate was signed and dated by the artist. Today collectors can still find bowls, teacups, or whatever in wonderful designs without forking out too much dough.

Art Nouveau furniture was rarely made by machines. Its flowing lines were too difficult for mass production. Once in awhile you may find a factory piece that has a little of Art Nouveau's flourish. It usually is a glued-on wooden carving depicting lilies or peonies. When new that would be the type of piece Carson's would have sold.

During World War I the Art Nouveau style—both stages— fell from grace. Its highly strung ornateness grew old quickly. Adapting Art Nouveau designs to factory production was not very profitable. The marvels of machinery in an ever-increasing urban society demanded an art more adaptable to industrialization. Then the next big trend, Art Deco, arrived. Never underestimate the theory of change for its own sake since people not only like but need variety. It is like the cycle of straight legs versus bell bottoms on slacks.

Ironically, Art Nouveau craftsman started the revolutionary idea of technology linked to art. Tiffany sheathing the light bulb in art glass, and Sullivan fancifying the front of Carson's are examples of an early union of art and science. High-tech wonders being embellished by art.

By the 1920s, Art Nouveau items were considered passe by the wealthy followers of trends who graduated to Art Deco. Treasure hunters in the 1940s or 1950s rummaged attics to rescue long-neglected Tiffany lamps and other sleeping treasures. Then in the 1960s Art Nouveau made a comeback and is more fashionable now than ever.

How wonderful that the Ritz Hotels in London and Paris and Carson, Pirie, Scott in Chicago shine as eternal Art Nouveau superstars. Whether by the artisans from Art Nouveau's first stage, such as Tiffany or Galle, or from its second such as Roseville or Carnival glass, Art Nouveau still adds flowing opulence to our lives.

The Arts and Crafts Movement

The Industrial Revolution was growing by leaps and bounds during the final years of Queen Victoria's rule. Its technological advances were generally considered beneficial. However, some artisans in Britain, France—and eventually in the United States—scorned what others considered progress. As a result of this thumbs-down verdict, the British Arts and Crafts Exhibition Society was created in 1888. Its doctrine encouraged a return to the pre-machine age values of quality and handcraftsmanship.

The Arts and Crafts Movement, as it is called today, was not a style, but a belief in the importance of quality and handcraftsmanship. Furnishings by the 1800s, whether Rococo Revival, Eastlake, or Renaissance Revival, were mainly crafted by machines. Keep in mind that the Arts and Crafts Movement was an informal organization of artists who made items in various designs but always by hand. The main styles of the Arts and Crafts Movement are: Aesthetic Movement, Art Nouveau, and Craftsman/Mission.

The Aesthetic Movement and Art Nouveau, as you now know, were both quite upscale and handmade. Only a few items from the second level of Art Nouveau had been factory produced. As Art Nouveau had two stages, so did the Arts and Crafts Movement.

There were many members, but one English designer became its most distinguished spokesperson. William Morris

Photograph courtesy of Skinner, Inc.

The number-one chair of the Arts and Crafts Movement is the Morris Chair. With it adjustable back invented by William Morris and made eternally famous by Gustave Stickley. This oak one dates from about 1907 as does the armchair on the right.

(1834-1896) disliked machine-made furnishings. His book, *The Art of the People*, published in 1879, stated his goal of producing an "art made by the people, and for the people, as a happiness to the maker and the user." His firm Morris, Marshall, Faulkner & Co. founded in 1861, was known for its handfashioned wallpapers and fabrics. Of course this was very high-end and not in reach for most.

Life certainly can have unexpected twists. Someone copied Morris's most successful design. The swiped version was easy to mass-produce making it more affordable than the original. It became a big hit. For a time it seemed he was better known than Mr. Chippendale. Prototypes of his original were even sold in Sears Roebuck and Montgomery Ward catalogues.

You guessed it. In 1865 he invented a very cozy chair that some say is more comfortable than a Queen Anne wing chair or even a Windsor. Today's "Lazy-boy" recliners are a modern version of his Morris chair. Resembling a deck chair, its back could adjust to several angles. Eventually some even had a built-in foot rest that popped out when the back was fully reclined. Imagine the impact of this dandy chair. This was during Rococo Revival days when most chairs had stiff backs and tiny seats. No wonder his innovation eventually made Morris an antiques legend. The gentleman, who handmade his products, became forever famous because his invention could easily be machine made.

Morris chairs were mass-produced. This resulted in Morris' principles of quality and durability, the backbone of the Arts and Crafts Movement, to be well received. His ideas of honest construction and little if any decoration also adapted very successfully to the Industrial Age.

William Morris represents the first stage of the Arts and Crafts Movement. Around 1900 Yankee ingenuity caused this philosophy to enter its second era. Craftsmanship still ruled, but machinery became more involved. The goal was to make quality items under the factory system.

This inventiveness was supplied by Gustav Stickley (1857-1942), the most important American cabinet maker of the Arts and Crafts Movement. Around 1900, Stickley started manufacturing furniture. His Craftsman line was an appropriate name for a follower of the Arts and Crafts Movement. Although Stickley furniture was machine created, he agreed with Morris

Photograph courtesy of Skinner, Inc.

A Gustav Stickley oak settle or sofa from 1910. Imagine how modern it must have seemed during the last days of Victorian-era clutter and velvet upholstery.

Photograph courtesy of Skinner, Inc.

A circa 1907 suite of chairs by Limbert Furniture who obviously stole the idea from Mr. G. Stickley.

and wanted "to make furniture strong, durable, and comfortable, and to base whatever beauty might be attained upon sound structural qualities."

His furniture was usually oak, undecorated, comfortable, and durable. Pieces had a square or rectangular look. One of his trademarks was an honesty of construction meaning structural elements were visible. Pieces showed their mortise and tenon joints. These were usually where the top horizontal piece fitted

Photograph courtesy of Skinner, Inc.

A 1912 two-door oak bookcase by Gustav Stickley. Notice on each side near the top and bottom are the tenons which gave Craftsman furniture a rugged almost Medieval or handmade look although it was mostly machine crafted.

Photograph courtesy of Skinner, Inc.

Twin beds dating before World War I. Just as Mr. Chippendale had been copied, the same happened to Mr. G. Stickley.

into the vertical side of a bookcase. This was a medieval way of joining two pieces of wood. A tenon or tongue of one piece was inserted into the mortise or hole of another. Then a second, smaller hole was drilled for a peg that was pounded into place,

Photograph courtesy of Skinner, Inc.

The Lifetime firm, in Hastings, Michigan, made this 1910 version of a "Craftsman" settle. The manufacturer wisely added a back cushion to make it more appealing for the masses.

securing both pieces. Although fashioned by machines, this gave the illusion of handcraftsmanship.

Stickley's furniture started in 1900, the last year of Queen Victoria's life. He loved the simplistic Shaker furnishings and gave them credit for inspiration. His designs helped end Victorian clutter in the early years of the twentieth century. Stickley also followed the less ornate understated examples of the 1700s Queen Anne and the Eastlake styles. He had no carvings or any other decoration. This was atypical of Victorian-era furnishings. If upholstery was used, it was never velvet, as seen on Renaissance Revival, but usually practical leather.

From 1901 to 1913 Stickley's catalogues, *Craftsman Furniture Made by Gustav Stickley*, sold directly to the customer. In the furniture-making town of Grand Rapids, Michigan, Stickley exhibited his designs which promoted his name but also gave his designs to the soon-to-be Stickley imitators.

The Craftsman line was considered the best, but there were many knock-offs. It is similar to those pseudo logos of polo players on shirts copying the costlier maker. The same happened to Mr. Chippendale back in the mid-1700s.

"Craftsman" was coined by Mr. Stickley, but some clever manufacturer came up with designs called "Mission" or "Mission Oak style." Antiquers will often hear these two misleading terms. A concocted story claimed design origin was from furniture in the old Californian missions. This invented name stuck, and Stickley often gets incorrectly called Mission along with his imitators. The Craftsman designation belongs only to Mr. Stickley.

The most famous of the Stickley clan was the oldest of six brothers. Two of his siblings, Leopold and George, worked a while for Gustav. In 1900 they founded the L. and J. G. Stickley Firm in Fayetteville, New York. They produced Craftsman-type furniture. They also made Frank Lloyd Wright pieces and even Morris chairs. Gustav never approved of his brothers' use of veneer. In 1916 they bought Gustav's firm and ran it under the name of Stickley Manufacturing Company. Antiques from the Stickley boys are highly collected, but Gustav gets the biggest bucks at auctions.

Another famous American participant of the Arts and Crafts movement was Elbert Hubbard (1856-1915). In 1895 after his visit in England with Mr. Morris, he started his Roycroft Shop in East Aurora, New York. His specialty was Craftsman or Mission type furniture usually of oak with simple rectangular lines similar to Stickley. From 1905 to 1912 he also made versions of the Morris chair. Copper bookends, trays, inkwells, and books printed on handmade paper came from his shop. Today, furniture by Hubbard, often called Roycroft or Mission, is a highly collected antique from the Arts and Crafts Movement.

The furniture inspired by the Arts and Crafts Movement is more fashionable now than ever. Much applause is owed to Gustav Stickley. His early efforts at trying to declutter American homes through his Craftsman furniture was no easy task. By the early 1900s after sixty odd years of the too-much-is-not-enough decorating chaos of the Victorian era, he started the movement towards lower-keyed decorating. A famous decorator and other artisans also helped to end Victorian clutter as we are about to discover.

30

The Birth of Art Deco

When Queen Victoria died in 1901, the Victorian era was officially finished. However, the decorating tastes of her days lingered as late as World War I. There were several people besides Gustav Stickley who finally got the public to do away with most of the Victorian clutter.

Elsie de Wolfe, a famous American decorator of the early 1900s, called the velvet and the clutter from her childhood ugly. She wanted unprecedented restraint to avoid the overdoneness of Victorian decorating. Decluttering finally arrived by the 1920s in two different philosophies. The first followed pre-1840s decorating tastes as explained in our antiques personality test. The second involved the most modern (even after all these years) style of all, Art Deco.

As a result of Elsie's trend-setting decorating, quality reproductions of 1700s furniture became more popular than ever.

These 1920s and 1930s versions were more authentic than earlier Centennial pieces. Consumers wanted copies that were line for line and cabriole leg to cabriole leg identical to the originals.

No flourishing touches, such as mother of pearl inlay that were added to the Centennial versions, were incorporated in flapper renditions. Factories such as Berkey and Gay, Mitchell, Kittinger, Winthrop, and Stickley created beautiful replicas. These semi-antiques are from what is now called the Golden Age of American furniture manufacturing. Craftsmanship was at an all-time high because technology had also been perfected.

Photograph courtesy of Skinner, Inc.

Venetian glass continues to be made in modern times. These Leaping Gazelles" have captured in glass that lithe and speedy look that Deco artists loved.

The 1920s and the 1930s witnessed infatuation with antiques as well as passion for the newfangled. The 1925 International Exposition of Decorative Arts in Paris displayed ultra modern designs in home furnishings. It included ceramics, glass, furniture, silver, and other items. These designs were called "the Modern" or "the International Style" because its creators were from various nationalities.

These two names are confusing. Then in 1968 a Parisian museum exhibited some items from that 1920s show and wisely formulated the name, Art Deco.

Loomism: Consider Art Deco to be Art Undeco which helps you remember its underdecorated philosophy. Visualize the 1910 Art Nouveau Gibson Girl with hair piled high with an hourglass figure gowned in a billowing white dress. Now compare her to Clara Bow, the famous 1920s flapper in bobbed hair, and a short, straight red dress.

Several influences molded Art Deco. This style inherited an important idea from its artistic cousin. Art Nouveau wanted art for everyone, but its lavishness could only cater to millionaires. Finally in the 1930s, Art Deco succeeded grandly in fulfilling Art Nouveau's goal of embellishing life with art.

Shapes

Art Deco got its geometric shapes from Cubist artists. In the early 1900s, some painters in Paris depicted objects in their works in an angular manner. Pablo Picasso (1881-1974) geometrically diagrammed the call girls of Barcelona from different angles in "Les Demoiselles d'Avignon." Cubist shapes eventually appeared in Art Deco objects from skyscrapers to world fairs.

Colors

As the Cubists painted, the Russian Ballet performed "Les Sylphides" on May 19, 1909 in Paris. The dancers' colorful costumes shocked the audience. Soon those show-stopping hues accented homes. The paler colors of Art Nouveau and

Photograph courtesy of Skinner, Inc.

This wool rug was designed in 1932 by American Art Deco designer, Donald Deskey, for one of the greatest Art Deco structures, Radio City Music Hall.

This bronze statue either by a French or American artist done in the 1920s shows the undecorated look of the Art Deco style.

Photograph courtesy of Skinner, Inc.

Rococo Revival gave way to vibrant greens, reds, oranges, and blues first revealed at the ballet.

Along with those jazzy colors, Egyptian motifs were once again popular. In 1922 mummified Pharaoh Tutankhamen was discovered by a British excavation team. Objects from Tut's tomb (dating from 353 B.C.) influenced designs. Triangular shapes adapted from palm trees and pyramids were the decorating rage. In Los Angeles, Graumann's "Egyptian Theater" opened before the more-celebrated Chinese one. King Tut remains the most enduring Art Deco superstar. His 1970s record-breaking museum tour reinforced Art Deco's comeback.

Wright/Streamlining

Also another important player was Frank Lloyd Wright (1869-1959). This architect severed all links with past architectural styles. He is to architecture what designer Coco Chanel remains to women's fashions. Chanel freed women from bustles and corsets to the slender, unhourglass flapper. In 1904 Wright designed the Larkin Building in Buffalo, New York. The Larkin boasted central air conditioning and double-paned glass windows. He even had steel office furniture instead of the more customary oak. This building was in Wright's words, "streamlined," meaning he was stingy with decoration. It looked as if a magnet had snatched away all nonessential ornaments. Machine-inspired streamlining summarizes Wright's contribution to Art Deco architecture which others followed. New York's unornate Empire State Building shows streamlining at its most beautiful in true Wright tradition.

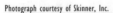

This server designed by Frank Lloyd Wright shows how streamlined his furniture as well as his buildings were of unnecessary ornamentation.

Loomism: Streamlining is like dieting to rid our middles of that spare tire.

High-Tech Products
A follower of Wright, Walter Gropius (1893-1969), founded the Bauhaus School in Weimar, Germany in 1919. He preferred high-tech products for his designs, such as steel, concrete, and glass, rather than the more usual wood.

Photograph courtesy of Skinner, Inc.

The ultimate Art Deco glass by Lalique, called appropriately, "Chrysis." It was intended as a radiator cap for an automobile. This French maker personifies the union of science and art that was very strong during Deco days.

Photograph courtesy of Skinner, Inc.

Although these Deco chrome and leather pieces date later than Walter Gropius of the Bauhaus School, they follow his example of using high-tech products instead of wood for their frames.

In 1925, Bauhaus disciple Marcel Breuer (1902-1981) patterned a chair with metal tubes as front legs. It was similar to Wright's office furniture for the Larkin Building. The Breuer chair is right up there with Sheraton sideboards and Queen Anne highboys as museum-quality antiques.

The Exposition of 1925 held near the Eiffel Tower showcased revolutionary designs. Art Deco displays of the first era were handmade, and of course, very expensive.

Of all the breathtaking Art Deco items highlighted, Lalique glass from France is probably the best known. It makes us envision flappers dabbing Coty perfume from Lalique bottles before doing the Charleston. René Lalique (1860-1945) became the most celebrated Art Deco glassmaker.

Designs at this show created a sensation, but it was not until 1927 that Art Deco came to America. Once it arrived on this side of the Atlantic, it never left. We are about to visit its most seductive spokespersons.

31

Art Deco on Main Street

In the late 1920s the French clamored for the jazzy Art Deco style. The geometric designs so beautifully crafted in crystal by Lalique were especially popular. Art Deco had practically taken over Paris. It was seen in everything from the facades of new buildings to furnishings sold at the Parisian department store, Au Printemps.

Then with a bang, Art Deco hit America! In 1927 when the French ocean liner, the *Ile de France* docked in New York's harbor, it created an artistic sensation. The ship literally introduced Art Deco to the United States. Its totally streamlined, geometric, and colorful furniture, china, crystal, and silver were a floating advertisement for Art Deco.

Manhattan stores soon realized this new style that bewitched New Yorkers would be a big seller. Trendsetting Saks Fifth Avenue displayed Art Deco delectables in its windows. Soon Art Deco, along with raccoon coats and bobbed hair, became the cat's meow for the swanky Fifth Avenue crowd.

Shortly after Art Deco's debut in the United States, the Great Depression began. As gloom ransacked America in the early 1930s, Art Deco entered its second stage. The geometric designs of Lalique and other Art Deco designers easily adapted to mass production. It also catered to middle American tastes and, of course, tight budgets. So factory versions of super-ritzy French Art Deco furniture became affordable for the average American.

Photograph courtesy of Skinner, Inc.

This famous photograph by Berenice Abbott (American, 1898-1991) shows New York in the early 1930s. Manhattan then was probably the most modern city in the world and ready to host the most technologically advanced World's Fair ever held. Manhattan skyscrapers put up during those days remain the greatest spokesperson for Art Deco.

How the beauty of Art Deco was needed during those tough times! Almost a quarter of the American labor force was unemployed, and then there was Hitler's threat of war. While all that raged, Art Deco began to embellish homes across the country.

Loomism: Think of the 1930s Art Deco as Main Street Deco because America became "Decoized." The depression decade was also the era of Roseville vases, metal smoking stands, and bedroom dressers with curved tops called waterfall. Main streets across America sported Art Deco-styled drive-in restaurants like the White Castle hamburger stand.

However, there was some fun during those trying days. Two world's fairs (one in Chicago, the other in New York) presented Art Deco at its best. They helped the world to pause from its troubles and to chuckle at least for a while. Attending those was as forgetting everything for fairgoers as antiquing is for us!

The "Century of Progress," marking Chicago's Centennial as a city, opened on May 27, 1933. While quite an accomplishment, it was even more impressive because it was staged entirely without government money.

Photograph courtesy of Skinner, Inc.

On the left are four aluminum plaques retailed in the super ritzy Georj Jensen store in New York. The center four glass are unmarked but really capture the geometric beat of Art Deco. On the far right, the ceramic plate by the Homer Laughlin firm was a souvenir of the 1939 World's Fair.

The fair's pavilons were decorated in Art Deco's gleeful and loud colors. They were similar to those at the 1909 Ballet Russe in Paris. Bright yellows, reds, and oranges glamorized many buildings. How invigorating this was for everyone. The displays heralded a better life, thanks to modern technology. The message was: "There is still optimism and beauty, and we shall make it!"

Chicago's Sky Ride was the fair's most fun spot. It transported passengers in cars suspended over the grounds. What a great view of the vibrant pavilions! How fondly my Aunt Panny reminisced about this marvelous attraction! Competing with the Sky Ride there was something that science could never replace and Aunt Panny would never mention. It was Sally Rand dancing in a totally streamlined outfit with only swirling fans separating all of her from the exuberant audience. While her costume was minimal, her salary was a Rococo $3,000 per week! Quite astonishing when the average secretary took home about $20 a week.

At the New York World's Fair five years later, Art Deco triumphed again. The "World of Tomorrow" opened on April 30, 1939–almost the eve of World War II. The huge fair was in Flushing Meadows, in Queens, a borough of New York City.

The site was in view of two Art Deco superstars—the Chrysler and the Empire State Buildings.

Ten thousand trees and one million tulips transformed a dump into an enchanting park. The New York Fair did not use the flamboyant Art Deco colors that had decorated the Chicago celebration but chose calm white. After all, eastern and older New York wanted to present a staid image, rather than a jazzy one that younger, western Chicago had projected.

It was in 1939 that scientific achievements in Art Deco packaging really caught the public's fancy. Attempting to forget bread lines and bombs, the New York World's Fair predicted a happy future. The General Motors show, "Futurama" by noted Art Deco designer Norman Bel Geddes, attracted 28,000 visitors per day. Another popular exhibit was the miniature display of a 1960 America full of 14-lane highways, slum-free cities, and circular skyscrapers. Even television made its debut at the fair. A demonstration of RCA TV sets really amused the curious public.

Johnny Weissmuller, the famous Tarzan from the movies, starred in Billy Rose's water show, "Aquacade." Although he left his loin cloth in Hollywood, Weissmuller wore daring (by 1939 standards) topless swimming trunks! Men's swim suits had only recently been streamlined of their tops. Mr. Tarzan had tough competition from the fair's official robot—the charismatic "Electro" who talked, smoked cigarettes, and totally captivated audiences.

Johnny and Electro were not the only attractions to draw long lines. Fairgoers also waited patiently to see "The Talk of the Town," a display of fifteen ultra high-tech homes ranging in price from several thousand to the astronomical price of $20,000!

Main Street Deco in Action

A streamlined tour of one of the homes shows 1930s Art Deco in action. We are visiting a model that has two bedrooms, a kitchen, a one-car garage with a brand new air-conditioned Nash automobile, living and dining areas, a utility room, patio, and one and one-half baths. Imagine, all this in 1939!

Art Deco streamlining dominates this spiffy showplace. Leave earlier 1920s Art Deco for museums. This house showcases mass-produced main street designs that beautified homes

Photograph courtesy of Skinner, Inc.

Quality Art Deco items by designer Russel Wright includes pottery vases, an aluminum bun warmer, and a covered serving tray. These pieces lacking any ornamentation date from the time of the New York Fair.

all across America. Mary and Russel (only one l) Wright (1904-1976) would love this house! Although no blood relation to Frank Lloyd Wright, they were certainly artistic relatives. Frank designed streamlined homes, and the Russels lived the streamlined Art Deco lifestyle.

In 1950 Russel and Mary Wright wrote *The Guide for Easy Living,* a how-to about streamlining life of unnecessary material things. Colonial, Victorian, and French styles meant too much work. Curlicues required dusting. The Wrights simplified their entertaining by avoiding china, silver, and black-tie attire. Their American informal lifestyle preferred grilling on the patio, disposable dishes, and buffet dinners instead of formal, sit-down affairs.

All three Wrights would appreciate the first-floor, L-shaped dining and living area similar to Frank Wright's great room. However, the kitchen is the show stopper, a "shining example of the machine," as one 1930s magazine touted it.

Even today, this kitchen is still mighty up-to-date. The only thing missing is the microwave. The steel cabinets circling three walls streamlined kitchen work.

The drawer by the sink holds a set of the stainless steel flatware so popular in Deco days. Russel loved inexpensive stainless because unlike silver and silverplate, it never tarnished.

To complement the flatware, the cabinets store two fabled sets of Art Deco china, "American Modern" and "Fiestaware."

American Modern sold across the country at department stores. The earthenware pieces designed by Russel Wright have the same geometric shapes as those that starred at the Deco fairs. Wright's dishes came in sea-foam green, granite gray, chartreuse, and others. Mixing colors in true Deco spirit created colorful tables.

Fiestaware in happy-go-lucky colors was the everyday version of the famous 1930s high-end English Clarice Cliff dishes. Sets made by Homer Laughlin were sold between 1936 and 1974 at Woolworth's on main streets across the country. Fiestaware, in flashier colors than American Informal, has concentric ring design and very thick shapes. It comes in yellow, red, cobalt blue, and that very Art Deco turquoise. They are being made again, so be careful when buying antique pieces. The best advice is to hold an old next to a brand-new to see the difference.

Outside the kitchen is the dining area, part of the great room. It is small because larger was not needed. There is a matching china closet and a drop-leaf table. No sideboard was necessary, thanks to all those kitchen cabinets. The dining set, of course, is decorated in a geometric veneer design in the manner of that famous earlier Art Deco furniture designer, Ruhlmann.

The living room is a generous 14 x 22 foot expanse, featuring a fireplace without mantle. Before Art Deco, mantels were the showoff places for collections of you-name-it that gathered dust. In Deco homes, they were done away with because that meant less cleaning.

A large pink bowl brightens the cocktail table. It is fashioned of Depression Glass, Main Street's less expensive version of the milky looking French Lalique. As Fiestaware, it came in a variety of colors with geometric designs.

Near the cocktail table is a smoking stand. Following the Bauhaus idea of using high-tech products for household items, it is aluminum. Henry Dreyfus, inventor of the one-piece telephone, created the smoker for that incredible Art Deco train, the "Twentieth Century." You will probably recognize the popular smoking stand—a pedestal topped with a doughnut-shaped ashtray. Its

Photograph from author's collection.

This bedroom suite was immensely popular all across the U.S. Sears sold renditions of it for about $150 that included double bed, dresser, and vanity. Its curvy fronts gave it the name "waterfall." It was veneered with mahogany in a geometric Deco fashion that had a brown walnut type stain. Today these are very collected semi-antiques that will soon become genuine ones.

spring device cleverly cleared ashes, making the smoker a popular 1930s gadget. Today, wise collectors use them as plant stands.

The master bedroom suite made in Grand Rapids, Michigan includes a dresser, mirror, vanity, bench, nightstand, and clothes press. A geometric inlay of dark and light wood gives the set that Art Deco feel as first created by Ruhlmann. The unique waterfall look on the front of the pieces attracted much interest. Nineteen thirties advertising described this furniture as "stream-lined, with the simplicity of modern tastes." Well put!

A Deco version of a small wardrobe is the clothes press. One side has a space for hanging clothes, and the other has a built-in dresser like the earlier Shaker version. This cabinet streamlined dressing time because it ended scrambling from dresser to closet for various clothes. It was so handy to hang on one side those 1930s Claystones shirts for men in Fiestaware colors and on the other side, place socks in drawers.

It was not just the furniture of Deco days that was stream-lined. The people were too! This is a good place to mention how

Art Deco modernized unmentionables. Cooper Underwear, in true Art Deco spirit, abbreviated men's boxer shorts into sleek "jockey" shorts. Today the firm is appropriately called Jockey Underwear. While males were being streamlined, females were getting a little figure control assistance. Women had "once-overs" which advertising of the day pointed out "hinders wayward curves while gently persuading your figure to lithe smoothness." In artistic terms they were streamliners. Women loved synthetic nylon, an Art Deco miracle invented in 1939 by Dupont Chemical. It quickly replaced costlier silk for ladies' stockings.

The bathroom is another example of Art Deco's "beauty in the useful." Its pink fixtures contrast with Ruhlmann-inspired black and white ceramic wall tile designs. The wall-mounted commode, invented by Frank Lloyd Wright some thirty years earlier, meant easy cleaning around its base.

The furniture in the last room, the second bedroom, seems out of place. What are Hepplewhite-style furniture and floral drapes doing in this Art Deco showplace? What would the three Wrights say? Its dissimilar decor reminds us that in 1939, two decorating choices existed: the traditional which included antiques and reproductions; and the modern Art Deco. Fortunately for us today both of those designs have matured as antiques or semi-antiques.

Houses similar to the one at the New York Fair still exist throughout America. Their easy living continues to streamline

Photograph from author's collection.

Remember not everyone was crazy about ultra modern furniture back in Deco Days. Some preferred reproductions from 1700s pieces such as this room setting with its Sheraton style breakfront.

This coffee/cocktail table, similar to ones seen at the Fair, is over 50 years old. It graced living rooms all across America and in true Deco spirit it is eternally modern.

Photograph from author's collection.

chores. More recent marvels like dishwashers and microwave ovens keep the Art Deco spirit alive.

When the fair closed, Art Deco lost a star. Its dazzle, however, endured. In nearby Manhattan, Art Deco skyscrapers kept the spirit of the fair soaring. The Chrysler Building and the Empire State Building are more seductive Art Deco idols than any museum display. These landmarks outlasted the depression, World War II, and the remodeling fervor of the 1950s and 1960s.

In 1930 the 77-story Chrysler Building became the world's tallest structure. William Van Allen designed the Chrysler, the first to be taller than the 984-foot high Eiffel Tower. The Chrysler's gray and white designs soared into the clouds. It had a peachy view of the "Mad Meadow," a nickname for the New York Fair. This famous building, headquarters for Chrysler Motors, was also a monument to Mr. Walter Chrysler. This man with his cars and Manhattan palace was a real American success story.

The Empire State Building, probably the most famous man-made structure in the world, is another Art Deco idol. Designed by architects Shreve, Lamb, and Marmon, the Empire State Building's streamlined beauty is subdued compared to the flamboyant Chrysler. In the movie, *King Kong*, this beloved edifice completely stole the show. When Kong in the 1933 movie climbed to its 102-story top, the audience was more bedazzled by its high-tech radiance than the fate of Fay Wray. It won the height war against Chrysler and kept the record for an incredible forty years. In 1971, the 100-foot taller and

Photograph courtesy of Skinner, Inc.

Furniture from the 1950s, often called "Danish Modern," continued the undecorated look of Art Deco.

blander New York World Trade Center became first, and a few years later, the Sears Tower in Chicago became for a while king of the skyscrapers (at least from a height perspective).

The Empire State and Chrysler Buildings teach more about the Deco style than any book. Their lighted tops are the Art Deco beat. While new skyscrapers go up all the time, these two still outshine them all.

During the 1950s and 1960s Art Deco continued in interesting ways as Danish Modern furniture, skimpy bikini suits, dishwashers, color televisions, ranch houses, and fast food chains. Even McDonald's, based on 1930s drive-ins, has Art Deco geometric arches as its logo.

Just as it infiltrated Main Street during the depression, Art Deco is doing it again—this time as semi-antiques. The style's reentry is appropriate for our times. With the costs of everything steadily climbing, there seems to be less money for luxuries. There is still time to get hooked on affordable Art Deco goodies before these collectibles mature into antiques with fancy price tags.

Now onwards to the most controversial subject in the world of antiques!

32

To Refinish or
Not to Refinish?

The debate over refinishing really divides antiquers into two opposing camps—to refinish or not to refinish. There is no definite answer. This antiquer shares a preference with a beloved personality. Her opinion will be revealed shortly. The controversy is often older than the antique that needs work. Purists say leave the original finish intact—no matter how distressed! Then the other philosophy insists that old pieces should be done over to make them look shiny, perfect, and practically brand-new.

Furniture that originally was varnished to show the grain should always remain that way. Despite decorating trends, never paint or "antique" a varnished article to renew it. That would hide the wood. Graining and color were intended to be visible and should be maintained.

If the original finish resembles alligator skin, called crazing, there is still hope. This is the result of too little waxing and too much sun. Wood is like skin; it needs moisture to protect its surface. Polishing or waxing helps finishes remain luscious. Over-heated homes or too much sun can cause a wooden piece to get sunburned or crazed.

The TLC approach can do wonders. Take a chair ready for a face lift into the back yard. Give it a good rubdown by using the finest grade of steel wool and a furniture polish or wax. Old English, Goddard's Bee Wax, or Gillespie are favorites. Many dealers sell their own mixture of turpentine or linseed oil that

If this piece with its small paint loss looks too distressed in your opinion, you will be happier with one that was originally varnished rather than one that was painted. It is perfect the way it is because it looks old in a terrific way.

includes "secret ingredients." Apply the polish or wax liberally on the steel wool, then rub over the wood in the direction of the grain.

Photograph courtesy of Skinner, Inc.

Wipe off after five or ten minutes and let dry.

Most imperfections are superficial, so this massage does wonders. Scratches are in the outer varnished layer and not in the wood itself. Usually caressing the piece with wax, helps us to know all its construction idiosyncrasies. You will learn, for example, if the carving is glued-on or handmade from one block. The piece has been moisturized rendering nicks less obnoxious. Your antique no longer seems junky but old in a lovely way. This enchanting look is known as distressing—the way antiques should appear.

Photograph courtesy of Skinner, Inc.

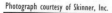

The moisturizing has preserved the old finish enhancing the patina. Patina, an often-heard word, is the

A beautifully painted cupboard from Pennsylvania dating from the 1830s. Whether this finish is original or not does not matter. Do not do anything to its surface because it looks old in a wonderful way.

The experts at Skinner's say the white paint is from the 20th century. That means probably underneath is the original 1700s paint. Take it to a professional to see if it can be dry scraped to remove the outer layer to expose the original surface.

Photograph courtesy of Skinner, Inc.

build-up of dirt and wax darkening the crevices in carvings. It gives character. Stripping wooden pieces risks removing the patina. It may take another century to recreate it. Why risk losing the deeper color around the wooden claw feet of an 1820s Empire table by refinishing?

When an antique from the 1700s or early 1800s still has its original finish, it is described as "original condition" or "superb state of preservation." This emphasizes that it has not been refinished. Thanks to its intact patina it is more desirable and hence expensive. An honest dealer will state if an item has been refinished, which will have lessened the value twenty-five percent or more.

Never refinish an originally painted piece. Some American furnishings made of less costly pine or birch never were varnished but were painted. If the paint is peeling, it should be repaired the same as a flaking painting should be repaired. Take it to an art restorer. Stripping will damage its quality and value. Removing original paint is usually impossible because it is imbedded into the wood's grain. Go to a professional.

Here are two conditions that only refinishing can repair. The TLC approach failed on an originally varnished gem encased under layers of paint, or its varnish is dark and deeply crazed. Refinishing is the only choice. Do not do it yourself; take it to a professional.

The purists may hate this verdict but the painted surface on this 1810 cupboard is too far gone to be saved. Have the paint professionally removed, see what the wood is underneath. It was originally painted, so a re-paint is appropriate, but if you want the natural finish of the wood, do it if it pleases you.

Photograph courtesy of Skinner, Inc.

Refinishing is an art that takes years to learn. Too many antiques have been ruined by a lousy job. What is good refinishing? It must never look redone. Its surface ought to feel as soft as petting a cat or dog. Some of those shadings around carvings should be undisturbed retaining some patina. When antiquing, touch a newly done piece. You will be amazed. Only five percent of most refinishing is top drawer. That is why only a professional should do the job. Word of mouth is the best source to find a capable one. Then check on some of his or her work. Remember the pet test. The new finish should be cat or dog soft.

Too many antiques have been ruined by poor refinishing. They are antiques, so why remove their aged looks? Buy brand-new if you want something shiny and fresh.

If you are not totally convinced about avoiding most refinishing, let Lucy Ricardo sway you. During one show, Ethel and she watched the movers unloading their neighbor's furniture. Lucy explained how antiques should have a less-than-perfect condition when she commented on her new neighbor's belongings: "She either has beat-up furniture or antiques."

33

The Antique of Your Dreams

I hope *Is It Antique Yet?* has hooked you forever on antiques and has started your foundation of knowledge. There will be no more sermons about antiques as an investment in beauty, their quality, or how they give us more for our bucks. Nor will there be any more explanations about cabriole legs, rococo carving, or the lure of patina.

However, one more thing needs to be reemphasized. The most important reason to love antiques has to do with our hearts. That organ famous for its emotions knows the best explanation of all for antiques worship. It does not matter if yours includes rare Persian carpets or Depression Glass bowls, the reason to collect antiques is the same. They soothe and bring us happiness. Every time you look at yours, they make you chuckle or smile, right?

As an appraiser of antiques I am always aware of their increases in value and status. Certainly an 1800s rocking chair or a Wedgwood blue and white teapot can really "class up" a place. That's all very nice but our hearts have the best reason for their veneration. Here is this antiquer's story of how the antique of my dreams came to me at one of the lowest and scariest times of my life.

A few years ago, I had a reoccurring hernia requiring a second operation. There were complications: a hematoma gave my stomach a bow front that looks great on a 1790s Hepplewhite chest of drawers, but not on a gentleman. There were other problems that are not necessary to explain only to say they added greatly to my depression after the surgery.

Every June the Midwest has a terrific antiques show, Heartland, about an hour's drive from home, in Richmond, Indiana. Considering the recent events, it was an even bigger treat to get to go that year. Antiquing is one of the great joys of life. It gives us a chance to forget our troubles as we cruise aisle after aisle ogling the goodies.

My jogging pal and antiquer extraordinaire, Pete, and I decided to go to this show together. His wife Dianne stayed home to take care of their sons. Pete's tastes in antiques tend to be more country while mine tend to be more citified. If he is trying to get my goat he says I like bordello stuff which is sometimes true. My reply is from my Aunt Panny who always said, "Everyone to their own taste said the little old lady who kissed the cow."

Most of us probably have one possession that we yearn for our whole lives. For most of us antiquers, it is the antique of our dreams. Don't let me give you the wrong impression. I didn't need any more antiques–except for one. All my adult life I have dreamed of a cherry Queen Anne highboy. As you know these gems from the late 1700s are basically a tall chest of drawers with a top part usually of four long drawers and a bottom part containing three little drawers resting upon curvy cabriole legs. Not only are they mighty stunning but they are practical, too. That is a trait that my flapper grandmother would approve. All those drawers hold many clothes.

We saw a few highboys and checked their prices. There was a mahogany beauty that was about $8,000. Owning one's business is great. However, there are drawbacks such as no sick pay. That means no work, no pay. The asking price for that highboy might as well have been a million dollars since by then I had been off from work for over two weeks.

Near closing time, there it was . . . love at first sight. We diehard antiquers use a colloquial expression (which shall not be said here) meaning that I was in a lustful state for this stunner. I certainly was, because it was the most wonderful Queen Anne highboy I ever met. It was not delicate nor prissy looking which

Photograph courtesy of Skinner, Inc.

Fellow antiquers, a first-class Queen Anne highboy in maple from the 1760 period. Turn the page to find what this antiquer considers the most wonderful highboy in the world. Before turning the page remember that "Beauty is in the eye of the antiquer."

is sometimes typical of that style. It was robust with bowed, fat cabriole legs. Just like its future owner, it had scars and nicks. Those are called distressing or the kiss of time. It was old, and it looked it in an honorable way.

The sellers were Tom and Darlene Brown from McMurray, Pennsylvania. Darlene, totally honest, told me its problems. Remember earlier when I told you about buying married pieces and how a friend bought a married highboy. Yours truly is "the friend," and I waited until now to tell you so you would be more familiar about antiques and totally understand my joy. It was a married piece meaning both the top and bottom were old but were crafted by different cabinet makers. Each was originally part of another highboy. That beauty yelling at me consisted of a top and a base that had been joined together probably in the last fifty years. To make matters worse for the sellers but oh so pleasant for this tight-fisted collector, the handles were replaced.

All these flaws are drawbacks to high-end collectors but not to this Group II Antiquer. To me it was antiques perfection. That highboy seemed worthy of the finest museum and most definitely deserving to hold my shorts.

Darlene had a friendly price which she made even friendlier because it was the end of the show, and they did not want to haul the highboy home. Then Tom said he would take another hundred off, arriving at the final figure of $3,400. This was about fifty percent less than if the piece were all original. Needless to say my passionate stirrings grew stronger. Was this a dream or did Tom even allow me sixty days to pay for it? He did, and my friends, the Haleys, two superb dealers at this show, said they would deliver it.

At this stage I did not trust my judgment because I was highly emotional (more than usual) due to pain pills and antibiotics. I asked Pete what he thought, and he said "go for it." I told Tom I had been off work due to an operation and wasn't sure that I should do it. He said with compassion, "not to worry."

That kind man did not make me sign a paper. I put $500 on it and gave him my word. Then I asked if I could take the middle drawer with its fan-shaped carving home with me. He said I was like "the old New York antiques dealers. They would always take a crucial piece of an antique they just purchased with them. This was to make sure the deal didn't fall apart before the item was delivered." I replied I was not untrusting but with emotional eyes added, "I just wanted to sleep with it." That evening my dogs, Josiah and Rudi, and I looked at it all night long and thanked God. In the morning I wisely added, "I shall thank you again, God, when it is fully paid."

The following Monday had been a rough day. That afternoon I met my surgeon at the Emergency Room at the Christ Hospital to stitch up my incision to try to stop the bleeding. Being at the hospital brought back very vividly the operation. While experiencing all that nightmare, thinking about my new-to-me Queen Anne highboy made me realize this ordeal would someday end.

That evening the highboy was delivered. When it was placed in my room, it seemed as if even the severest critic from

Photograph curtesy of Peter Coleman of Perfect Exposure.

To this very grateful antiquer this highboy is the antique of my dreams.

Architectural Digest would approve. The salmon-colored wallpaper brought out the auburn tones of its cherry wood, and it was the perfect height for the eight-foot ceilings. When King Francis I of France brought Leonardo da Vinci's portrait of the Mona Lisa from Italy to his palace in the 1500s, he probably wasn't any more thrilled than this mending exherniated antiquer with his 1700s treasure.

When for the first time the morning sun floodlit that cherry piece, I knew things would get better. This antique of my dreams was the proof. I would do everything possible to get both physically and mentally fit and to achieve my goals. The publication of *Is It Antique Yet?* was in second position on my list after health. Thankfully both became reality.

The "Brown Highboy" has received several caressing coats of beeswax to keep the wood moist and glowing. Don't worry, the Browns got paid, usually in installments, sometimes as little as $100. The last one was made two days after the sixty-day deadline. The Haleys sold for me on consignment several no-longer-treasured antiques which helped pay for the highboy.

Even this morning, to pull open one of its deep drawers that slide out so effortlessly even after two hundred years of use, it is still a thrill to get my shorts from this Queen Anne beauty. Sometimes after a downright ghastly day, Josiah and Rudi, and this trying-to-be-less-highly-strung man, lie on the antique canopy bed and marvel at that highboy. Watching it is as renewing as observing our feathered friends banqueting at the bird feeder during a blizzard. My highboy says, "Treasure the beauty in this world. Be grateful and remember you had worse times and. . .lighten up."

So now you know this antiquer's story about the true joy of collecting antiques our hearts understand best.

Here is wishing you get the antique of your dreams during upbeat times. However, if you ever have choppy days, go antiquing, and maybe you will become the guardian of the antique of your dreams. Or, perhaps look an unappreciated one in a fresh way that will revitalize you as joyfully as my wonderful highboy still does to me. That is the joy of antiques. Go out and enjoy them fellow antiquers, guard them carefully, and remember to:

"Keep Antiquing!"

Frank Farmer Loomis IV

Frank Farmer Loomis IV

BIBLIOGRAPHY

Aikman, Lonelle, *The Living White House,* revised edition, Washington, D. C: National Geographic Society, 1987

Aldridge, Eileen, *Porcelain,* Grosset and Dunlap, New York: 1970

Bates, Elizabeth Bidwell and Fairbanks, Jonathan L., *American Furniture 1620 to the Present*, New York, New York: Richard Marek, 1981.

Beck, Doreen, *The Book of American Furniture*, London, England: Hamlyn, 1973.

Bishop, Robert, Wessman, Judith, McManus, Michael, Nieman, Harry, *Folk Art, Paintings, Sculpture, and Country Objects,* New York: Alfred A. Knopf, 1983.

Boger, Louise Ade, *The Complete Guide to Furniture Styles,* New York, New York: Charles Scribner's Sons, 1959.

Brunt, Andrew, *Phaidon Guide to Furniture,* Englewood Cliffs, New Jersey: Prentice Hall, 1983.

Bury, Shirley, *Victorian Electroplate,* Country Life Collectors' Guide,

Cathers, David, M. *Stickley Craftsman Furniture Catologs;* unabridged reprints of two Mission Furniture Catalogues, Craftsman Furntiure by Gustav Stickley and the work of L. and J.G. Stickley, New York: Dover, 1979.

Chippendale, Thomas, *The Gentleman and Cabinet Maker's Director, a Reprint of the 3rd edition*, New York: Dover Publications, 1966.

Cole, Ann Kilborn, Antiques: *How to Identify, Buy, Sell, Refinish and Care for Them,* New York: Collier Books, 1962.

Daniel, Dorothy, *Cut and Engraved Glass: 1771-1905, The Collector's Guide to American Wares,* New York, New York: M. Barrows and Company, 6th edition, 1950.

Delieb, Eric. *Investing in Silver,* New York: Clarkson N. Potter Publisher, 1967.

Drepperd, Carl W. *The Primer of American Antiques,* Garden City, New York, New York: Double and Company, 1944.

Garrett, Elizabeth Donaghy, *At Home, The American Family 1750-1870,* New York: Harry N. Abrams, 1989.

Godden, Geoffrey A. *Enclyclopaedia of British Pottery and Porcelain Marks*, New York, New York: 1964.

Higgins and Seiter, *China and Cut Glass*, 1899, the Pyne Press, Princeton, New Jersey: 1971

Husfloen, Kyle, *Collector's Guide to American Pressed Glass, 1825-1915.* Radnor, Pennsylvania: Wallace Homestead Book Company, 1992.

Kerfoot, J. B., *American Pewter*, New York; Crown Publishers, 1942.

Kinard, Epsie, *The Care and Keeping of Antiques*, New York: Hawthorn Books, 1971.

Linquist, and David P. and Caroline C. Warren, *Victorian Furniture with Prices*, Radnor, Pennsylvania: Wallace Homestead Books, 1995

Mackay, James, *An Encylopedia of Small Antiques*, New York, New York: Harper and Row, 1975

McClinton, Katharine Morrison, *Collecting American 19th Century Silver,* New York: Bonanaza Books, 1968

Muller, R. Charles, and Rieman, Timothy D., *The Shaker Chair*, illustrations: Stephen Metzger Canal, Winchester: Ohio, Canal Press, 1984.

Nichols, Frederick D. and Bear, James A. Jr. *Monticello, A Guidebook,* Monticello, Virginia: Thomas Jefferson Memorial Foundation, 1982.

Okie, Howard, Pitcher, *Old Silver and Old Sheffield Plate,* Doubleday, Garden City, New York: Doran and Co, 1936.

Osborn, Howard, *An Illustrated Companion to the Decorative Arts,* Wordsworth Editions, Oxford University Press, 1975.

Papert, Emma, *The Illustrated Guide to American Glass*, New York: Hawthorn Books, 1972.

Pillips, Phoebe, editor, *The Collector's Encylopedia of Antiques*, New York, New York: Crown Publishers, 1973.

Robertson, R.A , *Old Sheffield Plate,* Fair Lawn, New Jersey: Essential Books, 1957

Robsjohn-Gibbings, T.H. *Good-bye, Mr. Chippendale*, New York: Alfred A Knopf, 1944

Santore, Charles, *The Windsor Style in America Volumes II and I*, Thomas M. Voss, editor, Philadelphia, Pennsyvania: Running Press, 1992.

Sikes, Jane E. (Hageman), *The Furniture Makers of Cincinnati*, 1790-1840, 1976.

Stone, Jonathan Stone, *English Silver, of the 18th Century*, London, England: Cory Adams and Mackay Ltd, 1965.

Stout, Sandra McPhee, *Depression Glass Price Guide,* Des Moines, Iowa: Wallace Homestead Book Company, 1976.

Strong, Roy, *The Random House Collector's Encyclopedia Victorian to Art Deco*, New York, New York: Random House, 1974

Walton, Paul *Renoir*, New York: Tudor Publishing, 1967.

Wenham, Edward, *Antiques A to Z,* London: G. Bell and Sons, 1969.

Wills, Geoffrey, *Wedgwood*, Secaucus, New Jersey: Chartwell Books Inc., 1989.

About the Author
Frank Farmer Loomis IV

Frances LaRocque Lennon, Mr. Loomis' grandmother, gave him his first antique. It was the beginning of a lifelong love affair. Like all true passions, it grew and deepened through the years.

Mr. Loomis, a professional antiques appraiser in Cincinnati, is out to make antiquing the new national pastime. A recognized authority on antiques, he enthusiastically shares his insights, loves and joys through the media. He has written antiques columns for *The Cincinnati Enquirer*, and contributed articles for *Cincinnati Magazine* and the nationally published *Antiques Review*. He was host, writer and co-producer for *Is It Antique Yet?*, a television series on WCET/48, and is guest appraiser for call-in shows on Cincinnati radio stations.

"Antiques de-stress our lives," Mr. Loomis says. "They can be as beneficial to our mental health as exercise is to our bodies." He wrote and appears as host in the recently released **Is It Antique Yet?** videotape presentations: *Part I, Finding Out If It Is Antique Yet?*, and *Part II, All About Woods.*

Owner of his own appraisal business since 1977, Mr. Loomis has also appraised for Frank Herschede Company, a Cincinnati jeweler; and for Phillip, Neale & Son auction house of New York City. Earlier in his career he owned and operated an antiques shop for several years in Cincinnati, and also conducted estate "tag" sales.

A native of Chicago, Mr. Loomis holds an undergraduate degree from Oakland University in Michigan. He received his Master's degree in French from the University of Missouri, and began work on his Doctorate at the University of Cincinnati. He is currently an instructor on antiques for the Continuing Education Division of the University of Cincinnati.

"Antiques soothe us and bring much happiness," Mr. Loomis says. Always looking to spread the word and make antiques converts he advises, "I hope you let **Is It Antique Yet?** – the book and videotapes – be your introduction to the world of antiques."

Is It Antique A Yet?
The Video Series

You've read the book. Now see it in living color with the two tape video set!

Author Frank Farmer Loomis IV takes you on a personal journey through the pleasures of antiques.

Tape 1

"And the next time you've had a day that's less than perfect, see how the antiques lovingly soothe you."–Frank Farmer Loomis

Finding Out If It Is Antique Yet is a door swung open to the joys of antiques. How can antiques give life-long pleasure? Help you build friendships? Give off a positive vibration? The first video looks at how "antique" has been defined through the years. Mr. Loomis dares anyone not to see antiques in a new way after viewing this video. *On Location Video Productions, Color, 30 min.* $24.95

Tape 2

"I think that I shall never see a poem as lovely as a tree."–Joyce Kilmer

All About Woods will help you become an expert in the identification of woods. Want to know what your grandmother's rocking chair is made of? How about the chest of drawers in the auction yard? Cherry, mahogany, walnut, pine. . .each wood has characteristics that host Frank Loomis will differentiate in color and up-close. From the forest to the lumber yard to your beloved heirloom table, after watching this video, you'll know the answer to the question "What kind of wood is this?" *On Location Video Productions, Color, 30 min.* $24.95

Shipping and Handling: Add $3 for the first tape, and $1 per additional tape.

Special Offer: Buy both **Is It Antique Yet?** companion tapes and receive **10%** off the purchase price!

To order **Is It Antique Yet?** call **Alexander Books**™ at 1-800-472-0438. MasterCard and Visa accepted. Mail Check or Money Order to:

Alexander Books™
65 Macedonia Road
Alexander, NC 28701